SAN FRANCISCO

CITYSCOPES: a unique overview of a city's past as well as a focused eye on its present. Written by authors with intimate knowledge of the cities, each book provides a historical account with essays on the city today. Together these offer fascinating vignettes on the quintessential and the quirky, the old and the new. Illustrated throughout with compelling historical images as well as contemporary photos, these are essential cultural companions to the world's greatest cities.

Titles in the series:

Beijing Linda Jaivin

Berlin Joseph Pearson

Buenos Aires Jason Wilson

New York Elizabeth L. Bradley

Paris Adam Roberts

San Francisco Michael Johns

CITYSCOPES

San Francisco
Instant City, Promised Land

Michael Johns

REAKTION BOOKS

For Theresa and Dashiell

Published by Reaktion Books Ltd
Unit 32, Waterside
44–48 Wharf Road
London N1 7UX, UK

www.reaktionbooks.co.uk

First published 2018
Copyright © Michael Johns 2018

Printed and bound in China by 1010 Printing International Ltd

A catalogue record for this book is available from the British Library
ISBN 978 1 78023 921 7

OPENING IMAGES p. 6: view from California Street, with the Bay Bridge in the
background; p. 7: fire truck on Market Street during the Gay Pride parade; p. 8 (top):
Painted Ladies and park people; p. 8 (bottom): cable car on Powell Street; p. 9: Coit Tower
with Alcatraz Island in the background; p. 10 (top): Ferry Building; p. 10 (bottom): the Golden
Gate Bridge from Nob Hill at dusk; p. 11: Lombard Street; p. 12: view of church steeple
in Washington Square from Telegraph Hill; p. 13: people getting married in City Hall.
HISTORY p. 19: Golden Gate Park, 1967 THE CITY TODAY p.143: view from broadwalk to
Financial District and the Transamerica Pyramid LISTINGS p.199: Farmers' Market at Civic
Center with Federal Court Building in background.

Contents

Prologue: The Best Place for an Easy Life

"**S**he is all hills," wrote Gelett Burgess in his 1907 novel *The Heart Line: A Drama of San Francisco*, "they are a vital part of herself." Burgess was right. San Franciscans are always going up or down hills. They've climbed at least a few of the hillside staircases described in Adah Bakalinsky's *Stairway Walks in San Francisco*. They hear the constant whir of underground cables pulling wood-framed cars up Hyde, Powell, and California Streets. And with so much of the city tilted up and on display, San Franciscans see more of their city than residents of other cities see of theirs. The laying of a rigid street-grid on the city's irregular contours made its topography more vital still: when approaching by ferry, wrote Burgess, "the streets showed as gashes" against a "profile undulating in a continuous series of hills."

The undulating terrain gave shape to neighborhoods with eponymous names like Bernal Heights, Nob Hill, Presidio Terrace, Cole Valley, Twin Peaks, Cow Hollow, Potrero Hill, Bay View, and Hunter's Point. San Francisco's physically distinctive neighborhoods get their own weather, too. For the hills determine how and where the ocean fog enters the city. All summer long, the cooling fog edges onto the relatively flat western quarter of San Francisco. Sometimes it stays there; most days it either pierces gaps in the hills, engulfs the entire city, or slithers through the Golden Gate and across the bay like a huge, twisting, gray-white worm. The sparser, gentler fog of winter looks like pearly silk blankets laid upon the valleys.

Painted staircase at 16th and Moraga in the Sunset District.

"No other city," wrote Burgess, "has so many points of view." Or such a range of views, he might have added. For there are millions of short points of view from which you can trace, say, a line of bay windows ascending like a giant staircase up a steep city block. There are thousands of mid-range views, too, like the one running from Coit Tower through the church spires above Washington Square and over to Russian Hill. Hundreds of other views run clear across the city. From the southwest corner of Mission Dolores Park you can see all the way to the financial district. Or you can look west from Nob Hill to watch the winter sun set behind the steeples of St Ignatius Church on the hilltop campus of the University of San Francisco; when the light is right, the view is almost a religious experience.

The views from the city to its surroundings may be the finest of all. The Pacific Ocean sets the western edge of San Francisco, while the huge bay delineates its north and east sides. The bay changes color—from wine purples and pure blues to serpentinite greens and white-capped inkiness—with the shifting light, wind and tides. Just beyond the bay waters lie the hills of Marin, Contra Costa and Alameda: green in the wet winters, gold in the dry summers, and lit up by thousands of flashing-yellow windows at the end of each sunny day. While admiring the city from a spot on the bay in 1946—a view filled with cream-colored buildings climbing soft-looking hills—writer Edmund Wilson called San Francisco the "Camembert City". Wilson made his observation a decade after the city had spanned its waters with the long silver arc of the Bay Bridge and the vermilion streak of the Golden Gate Bridge. Their graceful power tempts you to see them as natural pieces of the landscape; at the very least they make you concede that human ingenuity sometimes improves nature's design.

If San Francisco is a physical beauty, so too is it a cultural pioneer. "Make no mistake, stranger," wrote historian Bernard DeVoto: "San Francisco is West as all Hell." What DeVoto observed some seventy years ago remains true today. For even though San Francisco has been a sophisticated city for a long time, it retains a frontier quality that has always attracted seekers—of fortune, power, pleasure, refuge, rebellion. Yet San Francisco is a particularly west-coast

version of the West: not just irreverent, independent, and a bit outside the law, but progressive, innovative, and open to all kinds of
people and ideas.

San Francisco was West as all Hell—in its special, west-coast
way—right from the start. Despite growing wildly in its gold-rush
years of the late 1840s and '50s, this instant city developed common-
sense ethics that kept order while encouraging liberties not tolerated
elsewhere. During the 1860s, '70s and '80s, San Francisco had a higher
proportion and wider array of immigrants than any other big city, and
it gave Jews and Catholics opportunities they couldn't find elsewhere.
As if to verify, however, the old cliché that every rule has an exception, San Francisco helped California prevail upon Congress to curb
Chinese immigration in 1882. Yet this rash exception to its rule of fair
play didn't stop the city from acquiring, by the turn of the century,
a reputation for tolerance, bohemianism and labor-union power—a
reputation enlarged by a stylish defiance of Prohibition and a spectacular waterfront strike during the Depression. After seeing the rise
of beatniks and hippies in the 1950s and '60s, the Grateful Dead's
Jerry Garcia said, "Things are always happening here faster and
sooner than anyplace else in the country." That was equally true for
the homosexual revolution of the 1970s and for the very first Burning
Man, who in 1986 went up in flames before a small audience on San
Francisco's Baker Beach—before becoming a mass spectacle in the
Black Rock Desert. Today, West as all Hell signifies "techies" putting
San Francisco atop *Forbes*'s list of creative cities, and it means resi-
dents of Bernal Heights and the Mission giving more money than any
other u.s. zip code to Bernie Sanders's 2016 campaign for president.

While San Francisco is justly admired for its hilly beauty and
West as all Hell atmosphere, its "everlasting appeal to all Americans,"
writes Lucius Beebe in *San Francisco's Golden Era*, "is that it is a city
that smells of money." Fried fish, briny fog, and roasting coffee have
perfumed the city since its earliest days, but the most intoxicating
smell is surely that of wealth. And the city has plenty of it. Most is
heaped at the top of the pile, but enough has always rolled down to
satisfy shopkeepers, longshoremen, and municipal workers—as well
as today's advocates for free clinics, affordable housing, and homeless

people. San Francisco's prosperity, in other words, underwrites the broad-mindedness so vital to its charm.

Money, beauty, and a West as all Hell permissiveness combined almost immediately to make San Francisco an easy place to live. With apparent sincerity, Mark Twain wrote this about an ordinary day in 1864: "The birds, and the flowers, and the Chinamen, and the winds and the sunshine, and all things that go to make life happy, are present in San Francisco to-day, just as they are all days in the year." (Twain went on to complain, of course, that San Franciscans failed to appreciate their good fortune.) Nearly a century later, photographer Imogen Cunningham felt a similar inspiration while working with Dorothea Lange and Ansel Adams at the California School of Fine Arts: "San Francisco," she said, "is the best place in the whole world for an easy life."

It's probably true that San Francisco offers the finest American mix of business and pleasure, nature and urbanity, competition and cooperation—and thus the best chance for an easy life in a big city. It's equally likely that no other American city thinks more highly of itself. Not for nothing did southern California journalist Neil Morgan once proclaim San Francisco "the Narcissus of the West."

HISTORY

Bosqui Eng. & Printing Company, *View of San Francisco, Formerly Yerba Buena, in 1846–7, c.* 1848.

1 Instant City

In August 1849 J. K. Osgood wrote to a friend in New York that San Francisco was "an odd place: unlike any other place in creation, and so it should be; for it is not created in the ordinary way, but hatched like chickens by artificial heat."

This odd, overheated place had been a forlorn Mexican outpost of 200 residents just three years before, when American sailors raised their flag in the square to claim the village of Yerba Buena for the United States. By the time Osgood wrote his letter, the place was called San Francisco and had 6,000 residents—more than three times the number it had had only six months earlier.

Osgood saw the products of artificial heat all around him. Each week he observed more masts and spars in the harbor, more boxes and barrels on the beach, more canvas tents and rough-board shanties going up the hills. He walked on unpaved streets that were dusty in summer and muddy in winter but filled with people as varied in nationality—Irish, English, and Australian; French, Spanish, and German; Mexican, Chilean, and Chinese; second- and third-generation American—as they were singular in sex: only 2 percent were women. And he watched prices rise faster than anywhere else in the world. A plot on Portsmouth Square that sold for $16.50 in 1847 sold for $6,000 a year later and for $45,000 a year after that. Money was everywhere, but the only important buildings were gambling halls around the square, and warehouses at the wharf.

So much, so many, so fast—and yet so isolated. The hothouse town that Osgood told his New York friend about had been "set down," novelist Frank Norris later wrote, "as a pin point in a vast circle of solitude." There was no other big town for 1,000 miles (1,600 km). There were no established farming communities. California wasn't even part of the Union until the end of 1850. There would be no telegraph connection to the east for ten years, no rail connection for twenty. And this faraway place was altogether teeming with nature. Massive salmon-runs flowed through the Golden Gate. Vast flocks of birds wintered on the huge bay. Pristine forests, grasslands and valleys spread far north, east, and south. To climb one of the town's many hills, and look for miles in any direction, was to behold what the authors of the *Annals of San Francisco*, a running commentary about the place between 1848 and 1855, called "one of the most peaceful prospects and pleasant sights of the world."

Gold was the "artificial heat" that made Osgood's San Francisco "unlike any other place in creation." The precious metal was discovered in early 1848 on the south fork of the American River. By the time Osgood got to San Francisco a year and a half later, it was a booming way station for miners heading to the streams, rivers, and hillsides of the Sierra. Yet Osgood had no idea how hot it would get. The town of 6,000 he wrote home about in August 1849 had 25,000 residents by the end of the year: an instant city of migrants—half from overseas, Europe mainly, and half from the eastern United States. Another 30,000 migrants, a good many of them Chinese, passed through San Francisco that year on their way to the mines. A few years later, the Australian traveler Ida Pfeiffer could write, in *A Lady's Visit to California*, that "San Francisco is unanimously declared the City of Wonders, and the Americans maintain" that it is "among the most wonderful things the world has seen." Pfeiffer was gently mocking the young city, but she couldn't deny that San Francisco had become a substantial place in record time. And just three years after her visit, no one could deny that San Francisco had needed but a decade to do what New York had done in two centuries: become a metropolis of 50,000.

Gold alone catalyzed San Francisco's terrific burst of growth in the late 1840s and early '50s. Merchants, financiers, and teamsters performed the hard task of getting imported supplies to miners in the Sierra. Saloon keepers, lawyers, money dealers, gambling hall

M. & N. Hanhart, *San Francisco*, c. 1850, chromolithograph.

owners, prostitutes, and real estate companies conducted the easier task of separating miners from their gold in San Francisco. But if these two tasks comprised the core economic purpose of San Francisco during its first few years, the young city was broadening its economy by the time gold mining hit its peak in 1852.

By then the city had banks, brokerage houses, law offices, wholesaling firms and engineering companies; coffee roasters, flour mills, slaughterhouses, tobacco processors, and whale-oil refiners; foundries, smelters, brick makers, ship repairers, and planing mills. Most were small operations that still relied on demand ultimately generated by gold. But they all belonged to an expanding urban economy with a growing geographical reach. Farmers, ranchers and fisherman now supplied San Francisco with a wide array of food, most of it from the Sacramento delta. Boats brought in slabs of redwood and fir from coastal logging camps. River steamers took people, provisions, and equipment to Stockton and Sacramento, whose merchants directly supplied Sierra mines and Central Valley farms. Speedy clipper ships cruised into San Francisco Bay carrying Manila hemp, Hawaiian sugar, Tahitian oranges, Javanese coffee, European wines and oils, Chinese rice, tea and opium, and New England apples, Pennsylvania iron, and east-coast migrants.

Just as gold stimulated the rapid accumulation of wealth in San Francisco, so did it excite a strange and high-spirited culture. "In business and in pleasure," wrote the authors of the *Annals of San Francisco*, "the San Franciscans were *fast* folk; none were faster in the world."

The first San Franciscans were certainly fast in business. L. M. Schaeffer lived in the city in 1851, when it had about 30,000 residents. In his *Sketches of Travels in South America, Mexico and California*, he observed that "everybody acted as though they had but a few hours only to attend to a year's business." *New York Tribune* journalist Bayard Taylor noted a similar quickening of life at the time. "The very air," he wrote in *Eldorado: or, Adventures in the Path of Empire*, "is pregnant with the magnetism of bold, spirited, unwearied action."

San Franciscans were fast in business because nearly all of them went there to make money to bring back home: hardly anybody went to San Francisco to start a family, build a career, escape persecution, or form a new religious community. And they all made long hard journeys. Some sailed from Europe or the American northeast via Cape Horn. Others sailed to the east coast of Central America before walking across the isthmus, where they waited weeks, sometimes months, for a ship to San Francisco. Still others sailed from Chile, Australia, and China. Most, however, took the overland route. They crossed the Great Plains, went through the Rockies, traversed the Nevada desert and negotiated passes in the Sierra—all on foot, horse, or wagon. One in ten died on the journey or soon after reaching San Francisco.

Living in a city coursing with gold (dust, nuggets, and coins) surely sped up the actions of these already acquisitive risk-takers. So did the rapid growth driven by the enticing metal: San Francisco grew faster in wealth and population than any other American city between 1848 and 1853. And because there were at first no farmers or manufacturers, the city depended wholly on imported goods that often arrived at the wrong times, or in the wrong amounts, and thus created repeated gluts, scarcities and wild price swings. Such conditions telescoped men's time horizons and explain why no other city had as many bankruptcies, so much land speculation, or such radical fluxes in individual wealth.

Henry David Thoreau made an example of San Francisco in a talk he gave in 1854 and later published as *Life without Principle*. He called the rush to California "the greatest disgrace on mankind," and said:

> The gold-digger in the ravines of the mountains is as much a gambler as his fellow in the saloons of San Francisco. What difference does it make whether you shake dirt or shake dice? If you win, society is the loser.

Thoreau exaggerated the extent to which modern economic life corrupted human values, and he failed to appreciate the liberating qualities of cities. But he correctly saw a link between the greedy hope of shaking dirt for gold in the Sierra and the greedy hope of shaking dice for money in San Francisco. Like the *Annals* said, San Franciscans were fast in business *and* in pleasure.

There's no doubt that a lot of people sought a lot of pleasure in early San Francisco. Gambling "was *the* amusement," according to the *Annals*. Letters, newspaper stories, and travelers' accounts all mention the primacy of betting during the first years of the gold rush, when gambling halls like Bella Union and the Palmer House were the grandest buildings in town. "The inhabitants of San Francisco," wrote the *Annals*,

> seemed to be one great horde of gamesters. There were exceptions indeed, and some men scorned to enter a saloon or touch a card, but these were too few comparatively to be specially noticed in the general hubbub and speculative disposition of the place.

If gambling was San Francisco's first amusement, women were its second. In 1852 there were only 4,000 females among the city's 36,000 residents, and most of them were as fast as the men—especially if they weren't married. The *Annals* described the numerous balls and parties in the many saloons and halls, where the most extraordinary scenes were exhibited, as might have been expected where the actors and dancers were chiefly hot-headed young men, flush of money and half frantic with excitement, and lewd girls freed from the necessity of all moral restraint.

The combination of so few women and so much money generated a big demand for prostitutes—nearly every other woman sold sex during the five-year gold rush—and it produced a rather coarse society. Because most men had no sisters, wives, mothers, or female friends in the city, many of them spat, drank, swore, bet, whored, stole, fought, and murdered far more than they would have had there been more women. In 1851 the *Alta California* newspaper was

> pleased to see that each succeeding steamer is bringing to California the wives and families of many of our merchants and mechanics . . . The happy influence of women in a new country is a great one, and we hope soon to see society established in San Francisco with all the pleasant *relations* that are enjoyed in our Atlantic States.

More women were indeed going to San Francisco, but it would be another decade before there were even half as many females as males. The huge imbalance favored the women—as seekers of attention, as sellers of sex, as searchers of husbands.

If life in early San Francisco was fast and free, it was also fluid and mixed up. Rapid growth, lots of money, a chaotic economy, tens of thousands of unmarried and ambitious men living in boarding houses and taking meals together—these were ideal conditions for a temporarily classless society. The *Annals* said this about the city's social structure in 1850:

> The great recognized orders of society were tumbled topsy-turvy. Doctors and dentists became draymen, or barbers, or shoe-blacks; lawyers, brokers, and clerks, turned waiters, or auction-eers, or perhaps butchers; merchants tried laboring and lumping,

while laborers and lumpers changed to merchants . . . All things seemed in the utmost disorder.

One trade that didn't change hands was that of launderer. With no women for the job, it belonged to the city's few Chinese and blacks. The speed and uncertainty of economic life in early San Francisco enabled men with little schooling or status to make more money than men of higher education and standing. Men from widely different backgrounds, by the same token, served together on volunteer fire brigades, played cards at the same tables, and had sex with the same prostitutes. In 1850 New York journalist Bayard Taylor observed that a "practical equality of all the members of the community, whatever might be the wealth, intelligence, or profession of each, was never before so thoroughly demonstrated." In his book *A Frenchman in the Gold Rush*, Ernest de Massey, who panned for gold on the Trinity River before writing for San Francisco newspapers in 1851, marveled at the "remarkable breakdown in social classes." As late as 1852, the peak year for gold, lawyer John McCrackan could write this about a city of 36,000 people:

> You cannot know the perfect freedom and independence that characterizes all our relations. Society if it exists at all is freed from the multitude of prejudices and embarrassments and exactions that control the Eastern cities.

San Franciscans may have been free of east-coast "prejudices and embarrassments and exactions," but they were never fully freed from their physical and mental qualities or their socioeconomic backgrounds. It was simply a matter of time before the city settled into a social order. In fact, McCrackan wrote his letter just as the city's economy was becoming more complex and orderly, and just as its lawyers, moneylenders, overseas merchants, and big property holders were starting to distinguish themselves from mechanics, clerks, store owners and, further still, from waiters, draymen, and gold miners.

In the year of McCrackan's letter, a group of merchants established a Chamber of Commerce while a developer bought land to build what would become, three years later, the exclusive South Park neighborhood in Rincon Hill. In 1853 the four-story Montgomery Block became the first fireproof building in a city that had suffered several big fires. The Block provided handsome offices and housed a law library, a swank billiard room and two dozen first-floor businesses that included a tailor, a bookseller, an oystering saloon, and two newspapers. Over the next couple of years, well-off San Franciscans founded the California Historical Society, the Mercantile Library Association, the Odd Fellows Library, and the Mechanics' Institute. At the same time, more people were going to the theater, joining churches, taking ferries across the bay to picnic in Marin and Alameda, and moving into new houses around Union Square—while sailors, laborers, and stevedores enjoyed lewder entertainments and inhabited ramshackle dwellings along a waterfront cluttered with piers, warehouses, and small factories. Although plenty of women continued to sell sex in 1854 and 1855, prostitutes were less tolerated in theaters and restaurants while brothels on otherwise respectable shopping streets were encouraged to move to second-story locations and put blinds in their windows.

The development of a recognizable class structure failed to produce, however, a corresponding maturation in the city's political system. Most San Franciscans cared little about politics, and most politicians cared little about the city. It's easy to see why. Almost everyone in San Francisco had gone there to make money to take back home. And even though San Francisco became an instant city during the gold rush, and its people began to sort themselves out by class as soon as shippers and manufacturers reliably made more money than draymen and prostitutes, it was still a frontier town full of young men. So even though more women arrived each year, and more people got married and joined churches and social clubs—even though more people, in other words, began to see San Francisco as their home—far too few of them voted, paid taxes, served on juries, thought about the city as a whole, or held their politicians to account. In a sense, the people of San Francisco got what they

George Fardon, *View from Stockton St. Showing Portion Bet. Washington & Sacramento Sts. 1856*, 1856.

deserved: a class of political leaders who, even by the standards of the mid-nineteenth century, were corrupt, cynical, and ineffective.

The city government did plank some roads. It underwrote the building of wharfs and filled in the cove below Montgomery Street, which became the city's commercial center. It also ran a police department and acquired east-coast engines for the volunteer fire brigades. But the city's politicians were better known for stuffing ballot boxes, selling nominations for public office, taking bribes for awarding government jobs, buying municipal property at discount rates, and failing to pay policemen for months at a time—in a city with a lot of crime. And even though San Francisco's court system worked better in 1856 than it had five years earlier, when it barely worked at all, justice was slow, crooked, and dispensed by packed juries.

James King was first a miner, then a twice-ruined banker, and finally a crusading editor at the *Evening Bulletin*. For about a year in 1855 and 1856, King used the paper to express his growing frustration with the city's ongoing political and moral failings. Other journalists had written about San Francisco's crime, corruption, and depravity, but King attacked with righteous zeal what he saw, quite literally, as the forces of evil. To his enemies he was an "assassin of character" and a "moral peacock." To most San Franciscans, however, he was, as historian Roger Lotchin writes,

> an unprecedentedly popular reform demagogue, and his political impact was devastating. He flayed the politicians, the prostitutes, the barbarous custom of dueling, the defaulting bankers, the gamblers, the toughs, the police, and just about everything in sight while championing the home, the church, the school, and reform—and the city loved him for it.

The city did love him for it; but nobody loved him more than the city's businessmen. For they had the most to gain by imposing order on a rich but unruly city.

King attacked relentlessly—often on hearsay, sometimes without cause. And he named names. One of the persons he named shot him in the street. King's murder in the summer of 1856 sparked the second coming of the Vigilance Committee, which had first established itself in 1851 after a spate of robberies and murders. The first Vigilance Committee set up foot patrols, held closed trials without lawyers, and hanged four people. The second Vigilance Committee followed similar lines but with greater purpose in a bigger city with more at stake.

Throughout the summer of 1856 the committee conducted warrantless searches, unlawful arrests, and secret trials. It denied legal counsel and the right of *habeas corpus* to the accused. It deported hundreds of people, including twenty politicians suspected of ballot fraud, and it issued death sentences with no appeal: four men, including King's killer, died at the end of a noose. But if the committee was illegal and used terror, it was no small conspiracy to take power. The committee was led by the city's wealthiest citizens. It had the backing of three of the four main newspapers. And it enjoyed the support of most San Franciscans. The *Chronicle* defended the committee, the likes of which no other American city had seen, by arguing that it "was governed by a higher law—the law of self defense by an outraged community." The demands of the people, in other words, triumphed over the obligations of the law.

The Vigilance Committee did not answer San Francisco's need for a legitimate and efficient government. Nor could it quickly tame the city's wildness or soften its coarseness. But it did signal to San Franciscans that they themselves had to bring about reform by becoming better citizens—by voting, paying taxes, and serving on juries, and by forcing their politicians to improve life in the city and perform their duties with a measure of honesty and competence.

DURING THE GOLD RUSH and for several years thereafter, San Francisco was the fastest, wildest, most money-oriented, and male-dominated place in America. Just as remarkable, however, was the speed of its evolution from a raw frontier town to a city with a semblance of order and stability. After noting that San Francisco had wasted its first years on "riotous living," the *Annals* in 1855 predicted that its "young hot blood will cool by and by." Just a year later—the year of the second Vigilance Committee—the literary monthly

John Prendergast, *Justice Meted Out to "English Jim" by the Vigilantes, San Francisco Harbor, c.* 1853, oil on canvas.

George Fardon, *Miner's Exchange Bank*, 1856.

The Golden Era made a more upbeat assessment: "That a city of the respectability of our San Francisco, could be raised in the short space of five or six years, appears incredible." The editors of *The Golden Era* took pride in photographer George Fardon's brand-new *San Francisco Album: Photographs of the Most Beautiful Views and Public Buildings of San Francisco.* Fardon's album was the first published compilation of photographs of an American city. While the views were more beautiful than the buildings, Fardon's photos did suggest that the former gold-rush town had a big future as a great city.

Mission Dolores chapel, 1856.

Mission Dolores

The making of California's 21 missions in the late eighteenth century was an ill-fated endeavor inspired by benevolence and right-eousness but carried out with paternalism and force. Misión San Francisco de Asís, now called Mission Dolores, was founded in 1776 by a group of Spanish settlers led by a friar and a soldier—the word and the sword. For half a century the mission's chapel, completed in 1781, was the centerpiece of a complex of adobe buildings surrounded by extensive tracts of fields, pastures, and orchards. At its peak in the early 1800s, Mission Dolores housed several hundred Ohlone Indians, the region's original inhabitants. If some of the Ohlone willingly learned the arts of farming, weaving, and animal husbandry, most resisted the imposition of Christianity. Many Ohlone had to be restrained from leaving the mission, and none became the self-sufficient and evangelizing Christians the Spaniards hoped for.

A decade after gaining independence from Spain in 1821, Mexico took over the California missions and broke them up. Small pieces of Mission Dolores were handed over to Christianized Indians, but most of it was sold off to local landowners or taken by Mexican officials. By the time the Americans took the village of Yerba Buena from Mexico in 1846—the first step in taking over the northernmost remains of Spain's once vast colonial empire—there were only eight Indians living on Mission Dolores.

The gold rush finished it off. The mission's various buildings were converted into a boarding house, a print shop, and several saloons, and a section of the grounds was turned into an arena for bullfighting. But the American government gave the chapel to the Roman Catholic Church, and the white, two-story building is the oldest structure in San Francisco today.

Cable car on Powell Street, 1896, with Hopkins and Stanford residences at the top of the hill.

2 A Town with Style

In the inaugural edition of the San Francisco magazine *Overland Monthly*, editor Bret Harte explained the cover image of a grizzly crossing the track of the approaching transcontinental railroad. "Take the bear," he wrote in 1868, "as the symbol of local primitive barbarism." The creature "has paused a moment to look at the coming engine of civilization and progress—which moves like a good many other engines of civilization and progress, with a prodigious shrieking and puffing—and apparently recognizes his rival and his doom."

Despite growing bigger and richer during the 1860s—thanks in part to its control of Nevada's lucrative silver mines and its insulation from the Civil War—San Francisco was still, as Harte implied, just a big town of 150,000. And Harte was right to think the railroad would wipe out the vestiges of gold-rush barbarism. For migrants now got there more easily, women went more willingly, and eastern money, ideas, and products competed more freely. Just as importantly, the railroad expanded the city's sphere of influence. In his 1901 novel *The Octopus: A Story of California*, Frank Norris shows the Southern Pacific railroad directing trade in every corner of the giant state—and throughout much of the western United States—from its San Francisco offices.

San Francisco nearly tripled in size between the coming of the railroad in 1869 and the catastrophic earthquake of 1906. During those years it was the undisputed capital of the west and the dominant port of the Pacific. All the while, its *Overland Monthly* magazine tracked the civilization and progress that, with all of its shrieking and puffing, turned San Francisco into one of the world's richest cities—and surely its most eccentric.

San Francisco's businessmen laid the economic foundation for civilization and progress by controlling the city's vast and thickening hinterland. They organized timber, mining, and farm operations throughout California. They ran a coastal trade in pelts, fish, and coffee between Alaska and Panama. They owned sugar estates in Hawaii. They shipped their factory goods all over the American west. And they handled nearly all of the west coast's imports and more than three-fourths of its exports. While bankers, shippers, railroad men, and manufacturers orchestrated the making and movement of goods from their downtown offices, ordinary San Franciscans saw the wheels of commerce turning along a waterfront worked by several thousand longshoremen, sailors, and teamsters.

On any given day in the last third of the nineteenth century, San Franciscans would have seen bay schooners, coastal cargo steamers, long-distance clipper ships, and tugboats nudging ocean liners into berths. And they could have watched a long line of Italian fishermen sail out to sea in what the *San Francisco Chronicle* reporter Will Irwin described as "lateen rigs stained an orange brown and shaped, when the wind fills them, like the ear of a horse." But the vessels most familiar to San Franciscans were the double-decked and broad-bellied ferries that transported people between the city, the several bay towns, and the state capital some 90 miles (150 km) up the Sacramento River. San Francisco was so dependent on water that the Ferry Building, situated at the base of Market Street, functioned like a rail station.

Just as the city turned its long, curving waterfront into a series of specialized piers, so did it arrange itself into distinct residential and economic districts. In his short story "South of the Slot," Jack London rightly declared Market Street the city's central avenue and main dividing line. The city, he wrote, was "divided midway by the Slot," a long "iron crack"—two cracks, actually—encasing the cables that pulled cars up and down Market Street:

> North of the Slot were the theaters, hotels, and shopping district, the banks and the staid, respectable business houses. South of

The first Ferry Building, 1886.

the Slot were the factories, slums, laundries, machine-shops, boiler works, and the abodes of the working class. The Slot was the metaphor that expressed the class cleavage of Society.

In reality, the city had various Slots expressing several class cleavages. The cable car was invented in San Francisco (in 1873) to conquer the hills. Nob Hill was its first victory, and quickly became a swank place for some of the country's richest capitalists: silver kings McKay, Flood, and Fair; railroad barons Crocker, Huntington, Stanford, and Hopkins; various shipping magnates, too, along with a number of big bankers, merchants, and property owners. The city's first blue book, the 1879 *Elite Social Directory*, listed nearly everyone on Nob Hill. Subsequent years of the *Directory* added most of the residents in nearby Pacific Heights. Like Nob Hill, the Heights were opened to upper-class settlement by the cable car. By the 1880s cable cars were also serving middle-class neighborhoods between Union Square and the new Western Addition, and running between downtown and the mostly working-class Mission District.

PUBLISHED BY CURRIER & IVES, 115 NASSAU ST. NEW YORK

	CATHOLIC ORPHAN ASYLUM		RESERVOIR ORPHAN ASYLUM ALMS HOUSE	
HUNTERS POINT	ROPE WORKS	BAY VIEW RACE COURSE	MAGDALEN ASYLUM	WOODWARDS GARDENS MECHANICS PAVILION ST LUKES HOSPITAL	TRINITY CH
POINT SAN QUENTIN		POTRERO	S.F. ASSAYING WORKS	HOWARD ST. M. E. CH. U.S. MINT CITY HALL SALOMONS HTL & OPERA HOUSE	LICK HOUSE UNION SQ.
LONG BRIDGE	MISSION BAY	S.P & C.P.R.R. DEPOTS & BLDGS RINCON HIL		MASONIC TEMPLE OCCIDENTAL HOTEL	
PACIFIC MAIL S.S. COS WHARF SOUTH PARK			SELBY SHOT TOWER	PALACE HOTEL COSMOPOLITAN HOTEL	
		MARINE HOSPITAL		GRAND HTL ORIENTAL BLOCK SEAMENS BE	
				OAKLAND FERRY, C.P.R.R	

THE CITY OF

BIRDS EYE VIEW FROM

AL PARK & RACE COURSE PACIFIC OCEAN, IN THE DISTANCE   CLIFF HOUSE   POINT LOBOS   PACIFIC OCEAN, IN THE DISTANCE   SKETCHED & DRAWN BY C.R. PARSONS.
CALVARY CEMETERY   CLAY HILL   LAUREL HILL CEMETERY   MOUNTAIN LAKE   PERSIDIO BARRACKS ~ MILITARY RESERVATION   POINT BONITA
REV. CHAS CROCKER ESQ. 1st PRESBT. CH.   1st M.E.CHURCH   HAYES VALLEY   ST.BRIDGETS CH.   FORT POINT   GOLDEN GATE   LIME POINT
ANFORD PORTSMOUTH SQ.   LARKIN ST.PREZBT.CH.   WASHINGTON SQ.   R.C.CONVENT   TOLAND MEDICAL COLLEGE   BLACK POINT FORTIFICATION
     POST OFFICE & CUSTOM HOUSE   ST. FRANCIS CH.   TELEGRAPH HILL   PIONEER MILLS
SAN FRANCISCO   SUGAR REFINERY   INDIA DOCKS   FLOATING DRY DOCK   SEBLY'S SMELTING WORKS

N FRANCISCO.
LOOKING SOUTH-WEST.

'Bird's Eye View' of San Francisco, 1878.

Lotta's Fountain and Palace Hotel on Market Street, c. 1880.

San Francisco quickly became a big, complex, powerful city, but what made it special, according to the great Bostonian Henry Adams, was that it "had more style than any town in the east." Nobody doubted the stylishness of its buildings. Countless firs and redwoods had been turned into thousands of ornate structures. What most people called "Victorians" were actually a set of related styles: Italianate, Stick, Eastlake, Queen Anne, and Edwardian. In his novel *The Heart Line*, Gelett Burgess describes their endless "scrolls and finials, bosses, rosettes, brackets, grille-work and comic balusters. Conical towers became the rage, wild windows, odd porches and decorations nailed on." By "wild windows," Burgess meant the boxy bay windows protruding from the fronts of most houses and apartment buildings. Banker William Ralston put 700 of them on his luxurious Palace Hotel. Like plants, San Franciscans seemed drawn to the light. Almost everyone liked the showy buildings and the distinctive look they gave the city. Few would have agreed with Burgess, who called it a "nightmare architecture," or with critic Ernest Peixotto, who complained in *Overland Monthly* that the flamboyant structures looked "cheap and tawdry."

If 10,000 Victorians didn't already give San Francisco more style than other American cities, its social iconoclasm surely did. In his book *Bohemian San Francisco*, Clarence Edwords called the city "the home of bohemia." He described its bohemianism as "the naturalism of refined people" who protest "against the too rigid, and, oft-times, absurd restrictions established by Society." The British writer and Fabian socialist Beatrice Webb agreed. In her *American Diary, 1898*, she observed that San Francisco

> is out and away the most cosmopolitan city I have yet come across . . . To the person who wishes to live unto himself without any pressure of law, custom or public opinion, San Francisco must be a Haven. If he combines with this "individualism" a Bohemian liking for variety of costume, manners, morals and opinions, San Francisco must be a veritable paradise.

Victorians on California Street.

Webb saw plenty of individualism and variety among the many writers, painters, actors, and musicians who lent San Francisco what Charles Tenney Jackson, in his novel *The Day of Souls*, called its "self-conscious Bohemianism." The city's journalists were self-conscious enough by 1872 to found the Bohemian Club. They soon let in artists and musicians. Eventually they relaxed their motto, "Weaving spiders come not here," to welcome free-thinking businessmen looking to mix with the likes of writers Frank Norris and Jack London; architects Bernard Maybeck and Willis Polk; landscape painter William Keith and poet Ina Coolbrith, who later became California's first poet laureate; naturalist John Muir, who founded the Sierra Club, and political economist Henry George, who wrote *Progress and Poverty*; sculptor Douglas Tilden, whose Mechanics Monument (still standing at Market and Bush Streets) brazenly depicts several strapping men working a punch press in loincloth; and journalists Will Irwin, a talented reporter for the respectable *Chronicle*, and Ambrose Bierce, who wrote satire for William Randolph

Ladies of the Barbary Coast, 1890.

Little Egypt, Barbary Coast, 1890.

Hearst's *Examiner*, a fizzy mix of gossip, sports, nationalism, and cartoons specializing in ethnic caricatures.

Bierce joked that San Francisco was "a moral penal colony . . . the worst of all the Sodom and Gomorrahs in our modern world." By all accounts, San Franciscans did seem to drink more, commit suicide more often, visit prostitutes more frequently, and generally indulge in more pleasure than people in other cities. San Francisco definitely had a huge vice district: the Barbary Coast was a ten-block section (covering parts of North Beach, Chinatown, and Jackson Square) dedicated to dance halls, brothels, and bars. The *Chronicle*'s Will Irwin called it "a loud bit of hell." Historian Herbert Asbury called it "a unique criminal district that for almost seventy years was the scene of more viciousness and depravity, but which at the same time possessed more glamour, than any other area of vice and iniquity on the American continent." Barbary Coast proprietors benefitted from the fact that San Francisco had more sailors calling it their home port than any other city in America.

While Clarence Edwords had good reason (in *Bohemian San Francisco*) to call his city "the pleasure-ground of the world," most San Franciscans took their pleasures in quieter ways than did the bohemians, sensualists, and frequenters of the Barbary Coast. In the 1870s and '80s, for example, almost everyone visited Woodward's Gardens, a mix of zoo, aquarium, museum, art gallery, concert pavilion, restaurant, and amusement park. Robert Frost lived in San Francisco until he was ten, and used a childhood memory for his poem "At Woodward's Gardens." A boy is tormenting two caged monkeys by hitting them with sunlight from his magnifying glass—until one of the monkeys reaches through the bars to snatch it. The monkeys looked it over, Frost writes, and "They bit the glass and listened for the flavor" before breaking it and letting it drop to the floor of their cage.

By the 1890s Golden Gate Park had replaced Woodward's Gardens as the city's main recreation spot. The park was a huge rectangle of greenery painstakingly coaxed from west-side sand dunes by civil engineer William Hammond Hall and professional gardener John McLaren. It was bigger than New York's Central Park, and nearly as grand. Visitors enjoyed lawns, meadows, gardens, lakes, walking paths, bicycle lanes, carriage roads, stands of Monterey pines and cypresses, an arboretum, an aviary, a Conservatory of Flowers, a Children's Quarters, and a Japanese Tea Garden. Off the northwest edge of the park, on a bluff above the Pacific, stood Adolph Sutro's ocean-fed "baths." Curving glass roofs sheltered seven swimming pools, an amphitheater, upper-level promenades, and natural science exhibits. Sutro's Baths were the world's largest. They regularly attracted 25,000 weekend visitors, most of whom got there on streetcars.

San Francisco's most widely shared pleasure, however, was probably that of eating. Everyone who wrote about the city wrote about its food. In his 1876 *Lights and Shades in San Francisco*, B. E. Lloyd marveled that "There are chop-houses, coffee-houses, oyster 'grottoes', lunch-rooms and restaurants in bewildering abundance in every street, lane or alley where are located a respectable number of business houses." Fifteen years later a Bohemian Club member

Sunday afternoon, Golden Gate Park, c. 1902.

asked, rhetorically, in *The Inner Man: Good Things to Eat and Drink and Where to Get Them*, "Do we over-eat in San Francisco? Has the number, excellence and cheapness of our restaurants inculcated this sin?" At the turn of the century, reporter Will Irwin thought the city's eateries gave "the best fare on earth, for the price," a winning combination that encouraged middle- and even working-class people to eat out regularly. Irwin particularly liked that most saloons gave a man a hearty lunch for the price of his drink. San Francisco's restaurants were supplied with a steady variety of fresh fish, game, and meat, as well as local fruits, nuts, and vegetables, and, by the 1890s, with Napa wines, too—all of them products of a Mediterranean climate that nourished a rich ecological system comprising ocean, bay, and delta interlaced with hills, valleys, and grasslands.

If much of San Francisco's "style," as Henry Adams called it, was fashioned by its ornate buildings, diverse pleasures, and many bohemians, so too was it shaped by its wide array of people. In his 1897 essay "Cosmopolitan San Francisco," Frank Norris suggested that the city is "not a people, we are peoples—agglomerate rather than conglomerate." That was true of many American cities at the time, but none more so than San Francisco. Between 1870 and 1900, San Francisco had proportionally more foreign-born residents—anywhere between a third and a half—than any other big American city. It also had proportionately more (and more powerful) Catholics and Jews. Unlike Catholics in other cities, San Francisco's were never dominated by a Protestant upper class. The city's Jews, by the same token, faced little anti-Semitism and counted ten of their people among San Francisco's hundred wealthiest residents. One of those people, Adolph Sutro, became the first Jewish mayor (in 1894) of a major American city.

But no ethnic group lent more style to San Francisco than the Chinese. In 1880 they numbered 21,000, nearly 10 percent of the population, and they lived in the heart of the city in America's first

Well-off Chinese
man with children,
c. 1890.

Chinatown street life, 1890s.

and largest Chinatown. No other "foreign colony," wrote Norris, was as distinct as the Chinese: the "Chinaman," he said, "is in the city but not of it." Norris and other Occidentals saw the Chinese as "in the city but not of it" because the men wore long braids and the women wore silk pants; because the men waged violent struggles for control of their women, more than half of whom were prostitutes; because the Chinese were neither Christians nor descendants of Europeans; because Chinese merchants sold opium and a good many Chinese residents smoked it. Norris worked this last aspect of Chinatown's foreignness into "The Third Circle," a short story about a young white woman who gets lost in Chinatown—only to be found, years later, addled and toothless in an opium den.

In *San Francisco: A Pageant*, Charles Dobie recalled the Chinatown he knew as a young teenager in the early 1890s: "Even if you were not a hoodlum, you occasionally threw a brick at a laundry door or called a vegetable-man a 'monkey.'" But Dobie's prejudice soon softened. Like thousands of other non-Chinese San Franciscans who did business with Chinese merchants, or hired a Chinese servant, or went to the Chinese theater, or read one of Chinatown's bilingual newspapers, or ate barbecued pork in a Chinese restaurant, or simply liked to walk through the neighborhood, Dobie began to appreciate Chinatown:

> we crossed Sacramento Street and in a twinkling were plunged into a new and strange world. To us everything was topsyturvy— the trousered women, the silken jackets of the merchants, the feminine slenderness of the men's hands, the fact that we could buy our firecrackers in butcher's shops. As the years went on and we returned again and again to the quarter . . . we grew to be unsurprised by the astonishing things that the most unlikely places disclosed. One might run across an exquisite porcelain in a fish shop, or a bit of jade upon the shelves of a tea mer-chant, or a marvelous head-dress of seed pearls in a place where hot roast pig was sold piecemeal in the early afternoon . . . We watched barbers adroitly digging the wax out of the ears of Chinese exquisites. We saw bankers reckoning their day's profit on counting machines and chemists in fur-lined coats grinding up sea-horses for a waiting customer.

Norris and Dobie described Chinatown in the 1890s, a decade after Chinese laborers were barred from entering the United States. Early sporadic bias against the Chinese turned into routine prejudice when thousands of Chinese rail builders moved to the city after the completion of the transcontinental railroad in 1869. The prejudice deepened throughout the 1870s as more Chinese migrated to San Francisco, wages fell for many white workers, and Chinese business-men took over the manufacture of shoes, cigars, and garments by paying low wages to Chinese laborers.

This is when working-class politics—part progressive, part mil-itant, part racist—began to play a big part in shaping San Francisco's style. When several thousand workers met one day in the summer of 1877 to show support for an eastern railway strike, some of the men turned the meeting into a protest against the Chinese. A large mob of mainly young Irish laborers went out that evening, and the next night too, smashing Chinese laundries and roughing up Chinese people. Four had been killed before the police, aided by a thousand volunteers, put down the agitators.

A self-educated Irish drayman named Dennis Kearney saw his chance to lead the thousands of workers who were ready to blame their problems on the Chinese. Kearney became head of the Working-men's Party of California in the fall of 1877. He held meetings on sand-lots at the edge of town, where he whipped up crowds with shouts of his rally slogan "The Chinese must go!" He even led a meeting of several thousand workers on swanky Nob Hill, where he complained about capitalists who employed Chinese laborers, and threatened to "lynch railroad magnates, thieving millionaires, and scoundrelly officials." After he'd been acquitted of inciting violence, Kearney promised to moderate his statements. But days later he told another crowd of workers that, "When the Chinese question is settled, we can discuss whether it would be better to hang, shoot, or cut the capitalists to pieces."

Kearney's Workingmen's Party was more of a social movement than a political party. It whipped up resentment against capitalists and the Chinese at a time when wages were falling, unemployment was rising, and bankers, railroad kings, and silver barons were building magnificent houses and riding in fancy carriages. The Working-men's Party won the mayor's office in 1878, but its bigger victory was winning enough delegates to the state's Constitutional Convention to write a plank against Chinese immigration. In 1882 California congressmen successfully sponsored federal legislation to suspend immigration of all Chinese laborers and prohibit the granting of citizenship to Chinese residents not born in the United States. China-town soon began to shrink, and would not regain its population of 1890 for more than half a century.

The Workingmen's Party quickly faded, but the number of strikes, labor unions, and union members grew in the 1880s. By the second half of the 1890s, San Francisco had the strongest labor movement

Emperor Norton, *c.* 1875.

Eccentrics

"San Francisco has rather more than her share of eccentric characters," wrote Samuel Williams in his 1875 essay "The City of the Golden Gate." "Foremost among these is 'Emperor Norton,' a harmless creature who firmly believes that he is the legitimate sovereign of the United States and Mexico." After losing everything he owned trying to corner the city's market for rice in 1853, Joshua Norton eventually lost enough of his mind to proclaim himself Emperor, dictate imperial decrees, and issue his own currency. For a quarter-century the Emperor spent his days at churches, schools, and civic events, his evenings at restaurants and theaters and his nights at lodging houses—all at the indulgence of acquaintances and strangers.

Frederick Coombs was also indulged. Coombs believed he was George Washington and stood on Montgomery Street in a Continental Army uniform, powdered wig and tricorne. Coombs vied with Norton for top spot among the city's eccentrics. When Norton tore down some of Coombs's placards, the fat, bald, and short Mr. Coombs accused the Emperor of being "jealous of my reputation with the fairer sex." Because Coombs had once been a practicing phrenologist, he may also have believed Norton was jealous of the size and shape of his skull. But in the end, Norton was the city's favorite: thousands attended his funeral in 1880.

If Norton and Coombs were *sui generis*, other eccentrics described by Williams were prototypes of future San Francisco characters. The Chinese herb doctor Li Po Tai, for instance, was a "prince of quacks and high priest of charlatans" who got rich by selling eastern remedies to credulous occidentals. A man called "Crisis" was an "American howling dervish . . . who holds forth on street corners" exclaiming radical ideas and peddling "tracts written in atrocious English." And "nowhere else," wrote Williams, anticipating the city's generosity towards its homeless people, "can a worthless fellow, too lazy to work, too cowardly to steal, get on so well."

of any city in the nation. At least a third of its wage earners were in unions. A majority of San Franciscans favored the right to collective bargaining. The city's archbishop even designated Labor Day an occasion for special religious ceremonies.

At the turn of the century, leaders of unionized workers won political control of the city. They were propelled into power by a failed strike. Late in the summer of 1901, the city's sailors and long-shoremen joined the teamsters in a bitter strike to make San Francisco a closed-shop city. Five people were killed, hundreds were injured. The city's most influential priest, Peter Yorke, sided with the workers, most of whom were Catholics, many of them Irish. The city's businessmen were divided over the strike, but a new group calling itself the Employers Association took a hard line against it. Most of the public discussion about the strike criticized the Employers Association for its resistance to collective bargaining while, at the same time, rebuking union leaders for failing to condemn attacks on strike-breakers.

The critical event in the strike was Mayor James Phelan's decision to let policemen ride alongside non-union wagon drivers. Although Phelan promoted civil service reform and even encouraged munic-ipal ownership of utilities, he didn't like labor unions. Phelan helped defeat the divisive and unpopular strike, but most San Franciscans condemned him for letting the police protect strike-breakers. And the mayor's action helped trigger a prominent unionist's threat: should the strike last long or fail, he said, "the men will take part in politics and work changes in the city government." That fall the new Union Labor Party declared itself for San Francisco's workers—as long as they weren't Chinese—and ran candidates for mayor and supervisors.

Although the party was made up of working men, it was run by Abe Ruef, a well-off and extremely smart lawyer who was about to become the first and only Jewish "boss" of a major American city. Ruef was more political opportunist than union man, but he quickly became the city's most powerful politician by backing the handsome leader of the Musicians Union, Eugene Schmitz, as the Union Labor Party's mayoral candidate in November 1901. Schmitz's victory put

Mechanic's Monument, Douglas Tilden, 1901.

a labor party in control of a city government for the first and only time in American history.

Several labor leaders, including the head of the powerful Building Trades Council, didn't initially endorse the Union Labor Party. They wanted to remain independent of party politics, and they saw Ruef for what he was: an opportunist who made Schmitz mayor so that he, Ruef, could advance his own political career by eventually making

Schmitz governor. Once Ruef and Schmitz took city hall, however, and after several successful strikes during their first term in office, the Union Labor Party enjoyed the full backing of the city's unions. Schmitz was reelected in 1903 and again in 1905, when all eighteen supervisors were elected from the Labor Party ticket.

The Union Labor Party swept the elections in November 1905 despite newspaper articles suggesting extensive illegal payments to city hall from gamblers, brothel owners, and saloon-keepers. And that wasn't the half of it. Ruef had taken bribes from utility companies in exchange for granting contracts to pave streets, extend the streetcar network, and install gas, water, and sewer lines. He also took money for setting utility rates, granting liquor licenses, and supplying building permits. Ruef shared his bribe and kickback money with Mayor Schmitz and city supervisors. The Union Labor Party must have felt like it owned San Francisco when it took office for a third straight term in early 1906; but it was about to lose everything it had won in the face of the biggest disaster ever to hit a major American city.

3 Ruin, Resurrection, Resplendence

At 5:12 in the morning on Wednesday April 18, 1906, James Hopper was jolted out of bed in his hotel apartment. In the early dawn light the young reporter for *The Call* watched his window shatter and a wall disintegrate amid sounds of crashing bricks and splintering beams. A minute later he was outside in the dust-filled air, where half-clad people stood like "speechless idiots." He walked to the Call Building, the city's tallest skyscraper; it was undamaged. But several nearby buildings had collapsed and many others were cracked. Hopper walked south of Market Street into a working-class district whose "frail shanties went down like card houses." He knew then that the city had been badly bruised. When he saw the flames, however, he also "knew that the earthquake had been but a prelude, and that the tragedy was to be written in fire."

Hopper climbed a hill to watch the blaze "spread its heaving red sea, and with a roar it was rushing on, its advance below cutting like a monstrous comber above a flotsam of fleeing humanity." By late morning the fifteen-story Call Building "was glowing like a phosphorescent worm. Cataracts of pulverized fire poured out of the thousand windows." By early afternoon the entire area south of Market Street was "one great flame, which smacked in the wind like the stupendous silken flag of some cosmic anarchy." Later that day the fire blazed through Chinatown before climbing Nob Hill, where it engulfed mansions, apartment buildings, and the nearly finished Fairmont Hotel.

All night long Hopper watched the city burn with a coppery glow, and he listened to the steady booms of dynamite set off by

San Francisco on fire with Ferry Building in foreground, 1906.

firefighters razing buildings in the hope of removing fuel from the paths of the fires. Throughout the next day he watched the fires gut several more neighborhoods while tens of thousands of people carried trunks, boxes, and babies out of the city. By the end of that second day "a heavy, brooding silence lay. And really there was nothing else. Contortion of stone, smoke of destruction, and a great silence—that was all."

Two-thirds of the city's housing stock, most of its factory district, and nearly every downtown building—some 28,000 structures in all—had been shaken or burned to the ground. More than 6 billion bricks are estimated to have fallen, some 3,000 people are thought to have died. Three days after the quake, the *Chronicle* published a letter from one of the 150,000 persons who had been made instantly homeless. "The spirit of the people," said the man, "will consummate the rebuilding of the great city in swifter fashion than any great city has been built or rebuilt before." What sounded like the childish hope of a desperate man turned out to be true.

Mayor Schmitz, who had been weakened by ongoing reports of corruption in his Union Labor Party, immediately appointed a special committee to lead the relief effort. Schmitz picked former mayor James Phelan to head the committee, which was composed of entrepreneurs, civic leaders, and newspapermen—but not a single member of Schmitz's Board of Supervisors. With no legal basis, the committee took over the governance of San Francisco from a discredited administration. And it went right to work.

By Sunday, 300 plumbers were fixing sewer and water pipes. A week later the city was serving 250,000 meals per day while housing 50,000 refugees in tents. Another 25,000 people were staying with friends or relatives. Seventy thousand had fled the city. By the middle of May streetcars were running on Market Street. When Hopper's account of the earthquake came out in early June—as "Our San Francisco" in *Everybody's Magazine*—several banks were open for business. By July the staff of the *Chronicle* had returned to its steel-framed building on Market Street. A month later cable cars were climbing Nob Hill. By summer's end some 15,000 horses had been worked to death hauling rubble.

Just as the city began to rebuild, however, its Union Labor government came to ruin. In October 1906 a grand jury indicted political boss Abe Ruef and Mayor Eugene Schmitz for taking bribes from utility companies in exchange for franchises and licenses. The

Days after the earthquake and firestorm, 1906.

prosecution was funded by a wealthy businessman, it was promoted by a reformist newspaper editor, and it was conducted by a prominent federal lawyer who worked for free while on loan from President Roosevelt. During the lengthy trials, the newspaper editor was kidnapped, the prosecutor was shot in the face in court, the house of a key witness was dynamited, the chief of police died under strange circumstances, and the entire Board of Supervisors (all from the Union Labor Party) resigned in a deal to avoid prosecution after giving evidence against Ruef and Schmitz. In May 1907 Ruef pleaded guilty to most of the charges while incriminating Schmitz. A month later Schmitz was convicted of extortion and forced from office. As the trials wound down, 1,500 members of the Carmen's Union went on strike. Before the strike was broken in November, fighting between strikers and strike-breakers left six men dead; streetcar accidents killed another twenty.

The trials and the strike got most of a year's headlines, but the real story was the resurrection of the city. By the summer of 1907 streetcar lines had been replaced, damaged structures had been repaired, and thousands of new houses and apartment buildings were under construction. During that first year of rebuilding, millions of bricks were kilned; miles of new gas and water lines were laid; huge stands of felled fir and redwood were shipped to the city; and 15,000 carpenters, framers, and bricklayers sawed, nailed, and troweled six days per week.

The manic pace continued for two more years. By the fall of 1909, 20,000 buildings had been erected and more people were living in the city than before the earthquake. A number of vacant lots and half-finished buildings didn't deter San Francisco from celebrating its speedy recovery with a five-day party called the Portolá Festival.

James Rolph helped organize it. Rolph had worked his way up from neighborhood newsboy to downtown office courier to co-owner of a major shipping company by the time he turned thirty at the turn of the century. He had made enough money, and had demonstrated enough charm and ambition, to be elected president of the Merchants' Exchange by the time of the earthquake. On the day of the quake itself, Rolph formed the Mission Relief Association, which provided more cots, food, and blankets than any other aid group. Five years after setting up his relief association, and two years after organizing the Portolá Festival, Rolph ran for mayor. "I will be mayor of the whole city," he promised in 1911, "and not the mayor for any particular section." San Franciscans welcomed his attitude after a decade filled with two long violent strikes, a brazenly dishonest Union Labor government, and big utility companies paying bribes for contracts. Rolph won the election and kept his promise. A journalist for *Sunset* magazine described him as a "keep-in-the-middle-of-the-road man . . . an avoid-all-needless-friction man." But Rolph wasn't merely conciliatory: he was also progressive, practical, and caring. He supported labor unions but distrusted political militants. He inaugurated the nation's first municipally owned streetcar service, and he initiated the damming of faraway Hetch Hetchy valley to supply San Francisco with water, while believing fully in the power of capital and markets. And he was open to all San Franciscans, including the Chinese.

Rolph was never better at being "mayor of the whole city" than during its big public events. And there was no bigger event during his two decades in office than the 1915 Pan-Pacific International Exposition. The exposition celebrated the opening of the Panama Canal, but it was equally a tribute to San Francisco's spectacular recovery from the earthquake.

Rolph opened the exposition by leading 150,000 people in a march of egalitarian simplicity—there was no rank or order—from city hall to the exposition grounds. The marchers came upon a delightful city-within-a-city that had been built on a big tidal marsh along the northern waterfront near today's Marina district. The exposition's landscaper built a tall surrounding hedgerow to suggest an agrarian past. Its architects put buff-colored, pockmarked, travertine-like plaster on classical forms to evoke antiquity. Its colorist enhanced the ancient look by using the tawny gold of summer grass, the deep cerulean of sea and sky, and the silky greens of oak hillsides to help visitors. He said, "Imagine a gigantic Persian rug of soft melting tones, with brilliant splashes here and there, spread along the waterside for a mile."

Hetch Hetchy valley ready for damming, 1921.

Water and Power

When Michael O'Shaughnessy became San Francisco's chief engineer in 1912, he also became chief engineer of the city's greatest public works project: drawing water and power from Hetch Hetchy valley in Yosemite National Park.

O'Shaughnessy said the politics of Hetch Hetchy were harder than the engineering. The city first proposed damming the valley for water in 1890, but it couldn't overcome widespread opposition. Much of the opposition came from the Sierra Club, founded in San Francisco by John Muir in 1892. (It is now the oldest major conservation group in the world.) Even after the firestorm of 1906 showed that San Francisco needed a new water supply, the politics of Hetch Hetchy proved difficult. Building a dam in Yosemite National Park required Congressional approval, deals with holders of water rights on the Tuolumne River, and the signature of the president. And it required overcoming the strenuous opposition of the Sierra Club, which had become a national organization. Muir wrote this about Hetch Hetchy in his 1912 book *The Yosemite*: "Dam Hetch Hetchy! As well dam for water-tanks the people's cathedrals and churches, for no holier temple has ever been consecrated by the heart of man." Yet the holy temple of Hetch Hetchy was eventually dammed by virtue of the Raker Act, which President Woodrow Wilson signed in 1913.

If the politics were hard, so was the engineering. O'Shaughnessy and his men first had to build a 60-mile (100-km) railroad up into the Sierra and construct a small powerhouse and two sawmills. Then they continuously poured concrete into wood frames for four years. After completing O'Shaughnessy Dam in 1922, and Moccasin Powerhouse three years later, they began connecting Hetch Hetchy reservoir to San Francisco through a system of (secondary) dams, powerhouses and reservoirs, 85 miles (140 km) of tunnel and 300 miles (480 km) of pipeline. Water and power from Hetch Hetchy finally reached San Francisco in October 1934. They're still coming.

Nineteen million people visited the interior courts—of Abundance, the Universe, and the Four Seasons—and their eleven palaces, including the Palaces of Machinery, Agriculture, Education, Transportation, and Liberal Arts. The structures were arranged along defined axes, built to uniform cornice heights, and decorated with fountains, reflecting pools, gardens, and statuary. Visitors marveled at a 5-acre (2-ha) model of the Panama Canal. They enjoyed displays of Samoan, Maori, and Somali culture. They admired Byzantium domes, Roman temples, and Moorish courtyards. And they were absolutely enthralled by a forty-story Tower of Jewels that featured 100,000 glittering Novagems: colored, mirror-backed, hanging glass crystals that shimmered in the breeze like the leaves of a cottonwood and, when lit at night, looked like swarms of colorful fireflies. The most arresting (and only surviving) structure was Bernard Maybeck's Palace of Fine Arts, where ancient-looking women turn their backs to the world to weep atop a line of connected columns. They "strike the minor key of sadness," said the urbane Maybeck, within the major key of progress.

If Mayor Rolph was better at attending public events—he claimed to have attended each of the exposition's 288 days—than he was at

Map of San Francisco, "The Exposition City."

Colored photo of Bernard Maybeck's Palace of Fine Arts
at the 1915 Pan-Pacific Exposition.

attending to legislative details, his real strength as a politician was
that of being a political mensch to all San Franciscans. In that spirit,
he was the first mayor to treat the residents of Chinatown as true
citizens. Its people still faced legal restrictions and routine prejudice,
but the Chamber of Commerce's 1914 *Handbook for San Francisco*
called Chinatown "this most fascinating city of America." More
importantly, discrimination against the people of Chinatown eased
as European Americans became less bigoted and Chinese Americans
became more Americanized. By the late teens, nearly all of Chinatown's residents spoke English, many went to their local YMCA, and
some attended services at the First Chinese Baptist Church and the

Chinese Congregationalist Church. And if most Chinese Americans still went to the Chinese theater, so too were they going to the polls—and Rolph wanted their votes. In the 1920s he campaigned throughout Chinatown in an open car with the president of the Chinese Improvement Association, and he addressed crowds in the Great China Theater, home to traditional Chinese opera. "During my administration," he told one such audience, "I have not forgotten that Chinatown is one of the most important sections of our city" which deserved to be "better lighted, with better streets and with ample playgrounds for children."

Chinese pharmacy, *c.* 1920.

Rolph did pay attention to the Chinese, but he was closer to the city's other groups. He became an honorary member, for example, of a women's suffrage association while running for office in 1911. Two years later he accorded to Rosh Hashanah and Yom Kippur the same recognition that the city had accorded to Good Friday. He went on to appoint Jews to important positions, and he became an honorary member of a synagogue. Because (the Protestant) Rolph knew the rituals of a parish Mass, and was a good friend of the city's archbishop, most people assumed he was Catholic. In 1916 he donated some of his own money to the financially troubled African Methodist Episcopal Church. Ten years later he served as pallbearer at the funeral of George Shima, a Japanese American entrepreneur who fought to repeal laws unfair to Asians. Rolph even invited Communist demonstrators to his office in 1930. And throughout his two decades as mayor, he supported collective bargaining, kept the police neutral during strikes, and was nearly as friendly with the city's labor leaders as he was with its leading businessmen.

Rolph must have known how lucky he was to be mayor in those years. The city grew in population by more than 50 percent during his five consecutive terms in office. San Francisco's Bank of America became the nation's second-largest bank, while its Pacific Coast Stock Exchange was second only to New York's Wall Street. The city's rail, power, and shipping companies, along with its diverse group of manufacturers, employed tens of thousands of blue-collar workers. Its central business district had the best shops and movie houses, the biggest set of skyscrapers and the largest class of doctors, dentists, lawyers, architects, and engineers outside of Chicago and New York. During the 1910s Rolph had the pleasure of inaugurating a new city hall, main library, and municipal auditorium. During the 1920s he presided over the openings of the Steinhart Aquarium, the Fleishhacker Zoo, the de Young Museum, the Museum of the Legion of Honor, and more than a dozen neighborhood branch libraries.

And because Rolph was humble in background, successful in life, progressive in politics, extroverted in temperament, and libertine in his appetites—he liked brothels, drank regularly, dressed smartly, and spent profligately—he was perfect for San Francisco in the 1910s and '20s. Rolph's San Francisco was that of George Sterling's poem "The Cool, Grey City of Love," which captured San Francisco's cool urbanity, its cool, often foggy, sometimes gray weather, and its bohemian love for life in a setting full of long views from bold hills overlooking a magnificent bay. Even the hard-boiled journalist H. L. Mencken felt inspired to write a flattering essay about the city. From high on a hill, he wrote in "San Francisco: A Memory," "the scene almost staggers. It is incomparably more beautiful than any view along the Grand Corniche" of the French Riviera. "No other American town looks like that. It is a picture out of the Orient—dazzling, exotic, and curiously romantic." It was not only the physical scene that staggered Mencken:

> What fetched me instantly (and thousands of other newcomers with me) was the subtle but unmistakable sense of escape from the United States—the feeling that here, at last, was an American city that somehow managed to hold itself above pollution by the national philistinism and craze for standardization, the appalling progress of 100% Americanism, the sordid and pathetic dreams of unimaginative, timorous and inferior men.

Mencken went on to strike Sterling's note of cool urbanity when he observed that San Franciscans "are stupendously alive while they are in motion, but they knock off betimes. The town is rich in loafing places—restaurants, theaters, parks. No one seems to work very hard. The desperate, consuming industry of the East is quite unknown." Fellow writer Kenneth Rexroth was to the political left of the older Mencken, but he agreed that San Francisco in the 1920s "had a tone that was unique in the Western Hemisphere."

The tone was epitomized by Dashiell Hammett and his book *The Maltese Falcon*. Hammett lived in San Francisco during the 1920s. For a few years he worked as an operative for the Pinkerton detective agency. At some point, according to his later companion Lillian Hellman,

The 1898 Ferry Building in 1915, the year of the Pan-Pacific Exposition.

he began to earn a small living from pulp magazines and squibs and even poems sold to Mencken's *Smart Set*. I am not clear about this time of Hammett's life, but it always sounded rather nice and free and 1920s Bohemian, and the girl on Pine Street and the other on Grant Street, and good San Francisco food in cheap restaurants, and dago red wine, and fame in the pulp magazine field.

It was, she said, "a world of its own."

It was the world from which Hammett conjured private eye Sam Spade, a street-smart and cynical lady's man who knew how to handle himself. Like Hammett, Spade navigated a dense world of theaters, neon signs, and hotel lobbies; of newspaper stands, lunch counters, and cigar stores; of streetcars, five-story apartment buildings, and elegant Art Deco skyscrapers; of sharpies, schemers, and gunsels. Hammett and Spade also navigated a world that got its tone—according to *The Spectacular San Franciscans*, a gossipy history of upper-class

Downtown in Dashiell Hammett's time.

life—from a "new type of young, highly nomadic, sophisticated, cocktail-bending, chain-smoking, wisecracking café society."

This new cocktail-bending time was Prohibition, and San Francisco handled it with more style than any other city. Six months into what would be a long, fraught, futile experiment in social control, San Francisco hosted the Democratic National Convention. Mencken wrote about it for the newspapers. He marveled at

> the humane and enlightened entertainment of the delegates and alternates. The heart of that entertainment was a carload of Bourbon whiskey, old, mellow and full of pungent but delicate tangs . . . offered to the visitors with the compliments of Mayor James Rolph, Jr.

Rolph belonged to the 83 percent of San Franciscans who voted against the Eighteenth Amendment.

Like most San Franciscans, Rolph believed the city needed not only its bars, but its brothels and betting parlors too. "San Francisco," he wrote to a friend, "is superior to any in the matter of controlling and regulating vice." Rolph was right. In fact, San Francisco's vice world was so well managed that it avoided the gangland violence that plagued so many cities during Prohibition.

It was managed by Pete McDonough, a childless widower with neatly trimmed white hair and bright blue eyes. He wore pince-nez glasses and tailored brown suits. He went to Old St Mary's Church each morning and gave a lot of money to Catholic charities. McDonough's father was a policeman who retired in the late 1880s to open the saloon that Pete (and his brother) would take over in the late nineties. The saloon was next to the Hall of Justice. City lawyers called it "the Corner." A graft investigator would later call it "the Fountainhead of Corruption." No matter what anyone called the McDonough's saloon, everyone knew that Pete was using it to run a huge vice operation in the 1910s and '20s.

Pete started his empire by paying lawyers, booking sergeants, and people in the District Attorney's office for information about arrests. He used his contacts and information to establish McDonough Brothers Bail Bond Brokers, the first such business in the country. The business became the basis for an enormous protection racket. McDonough paid cops, captains, and detectives for "immunity from molestation," which, in turn, let him sell "immunity from arrest" to racketeers, gamblers, bookmakers, prostitutes, brothel owners and, during Prohibition, to bootleggers and speakeasy operators as well.

Running such a big racket required high-level protection, which McDonough got by paying off politicians and providing free bail to union men arrested during strikes. When McDonough faced bribery charges in 1920, the Building Trades Council and the Metal Trades Council complained publicly that McDonough was being attacked by enemies of labor. In 1923 McDonough was caught selling drinks to Prohibition agents. He was convicted and sentenced to eighteen months. A number of important San Franciscans—including Mayor Rolph, three California congressmen, an appellate judge, four police judges, the police commissioner, the district attorney, the leaders of the San Francisco Labor Council, and the city clerk, recorder, and tax collector—signed an appeal for clemency to President Coolidge, who cut McDonough's term to eight months. He left jail as powerful as ever.

By the end of the decade, McDonough had amassed millions of dollars and made San Francisco's *Who's Who*, which said the "McDonough Brothers have a reputation of being honest and ethical exponents of the business which is their life's work, and their clientage is commensurate with the exceptional ability they have shown." Pete McDonough may have been an honest and ethical exponent of his business, but *Who's Who* failed to mention that his business was against the law.

Yet no other American city managed its vice in such a safe and orderly way. Criminal lawyer Jake Ehrlich's long career in San Francisco included representing the city's Police Officers Association, defending Billie Holiday against heroin charges, and clearing Lawrence Ferlinghetti of obscenity charges for publishing Allen Ginsberg's *Howl* in 1956. Ehrlich said this about Prohibition-era San Francisco: "Always a robust-minded town, San Francisco had convinced itself that vice was a necessary evil. There were many, as a matter of fact, who weren't nearly as convinced that it was as evil as they were that it was necessary."

Rolph was out of office and in his grave when a report about graft in the city's police department documented in detail what most San Franciscans knew in general: that McDonough ran a vast network of payoffs between the police and the city's brothels, speakeasies, betting parlors, and bail bond industry, and that he controlled a number of policemen who served as an "electioneering force" that solicited votes and raised funds for local politicians and union officials. The state stripped McDonough of his bail bond business, but the Atherton Report (named after the head of the investigating committee) admitted that the inquiry

> was not intended to be a moral crusade in the sense that it should bring about the closing of unlawful businesses, as such a course was contrary to the desires of the great majority of San

Franciscans. From previous residence in the city, we were aware that the bulk of the people wanted a so-called "open town" and that the history of San Francisco reflected a public attitude of broad-mindedness, liberality and tolerance.

Dorothea Lange, *White Angel Breadline, San Francisco*, 1933.

4 The Big Strike

Dorothea Lange was a successful San Francisco portrait photographer when the stock market crash of 1929 abruptly grounded the high-flying 1920s. When Lange lost customers in the first years of the Depression, she started taking photos of breadlines and street protests. Her husband, landscape painter Maynard Dixon, began painting pictures like *Scab*, an image of dock workers beating up a strike-breaker. Although San Francisco's strong and diversified economy spared it the extreme losses of jobs and businesses that devastated other cities, most San Franciscans suffered at least as much as Lange and Dixon. And like the two artists, they shifted their politics to the left.

San Francisco's waterfront strike of 1934 epitomized the city's economic slump and leftward shift. The "Big Strike," as it soon came to be known, was the most radical of the many strikes waged across the country during the Depression, the key period for union-organizing in American history. The Big Strike shut down the San Francisco waterfront for nearly three months. It featured two full days of pitched battles between several thousand longshoremen and several hundred policemen, battles that made the governor send in the National Guard. It hit its peak during a four-day general strike—the only strike of its kind in the history of the United States—that practically shut down the city. And it ended in victory for the workers, a victory that bolstered San Francisco's reputation as the nation's premier union town.

By the late 1920s, most longshoremen were fed up with the company union that had been imposed on them after a disastrous strike in 1919. The ship-owners ran the hiring hall, which the men called "Fink Hall." Many longshoremen had to pay off crew chiefs for work. Others stood in the humiliating "shape-up," from which foremen picked crews for the day. The Depression aggravated the situation by driving down wages and, at the same time, driving unemployed men to a San Francisco waterfront that was moving fewer goods while introducing labor-saving devices like pallets and forklifts. For all those reasons—and because the Communist International urged its American comrades to gain access to strategic sectors like ports and railways—the leader of the Communist Party's west-coast district made a push to organize San Francisco's waterfront in early 1932.

San Francisco was the west coast's biggest port. Its 2 miles (3.2 km) of piers could handle a hundred large vessels. The working waterfront began in the city's northeast corner at Fisherman's Wharf, where hundreds of small fishing boats sold their catches of crab, sole, and sardines. The long, curving stretch of piers between Fisherman's Wharf and the Ferry Building berthed ocean liners, cargo ships, and river boats. Each weekday fifty ferries carried 60,000 passengers to and from the Ferry Building, which opened directly onto the base of Market Street, the hub of San Francisco's extensive streetcar system. The biggest freighters docked along a section of piers that ran for a mile south from the Ferry Building. Beyond the piers were dry docks, foundries, a railway repair yard, a sugar refinery, pipe- and wire-making plants, and cement, lumber, and gravel yards.

Tens of thousands of people passed by the docks every day. Unlike today's container ports, back then you could get up close and see the action. You could walk beneath the prow of a ship, its cables and anchors hanging like watch chains. You could see sailors boarding, scalers scraping, mechanics making repairs. You could watch overhead winches lower crates, boxes, and bags into a ship's hold while longshoremen drove pallet-pulling jitneys between the storage shed and dock apron. You could look through the huge door of a pier to see row after row of high-stacked goods, and then turn around to see trucks and trains rolling up and down the waterfront. Across the wide street from the docks you would have seen a zone of bars, pool halls, tattoo parlors, cheap hotels, warehouses, small factories, lunch rooms, wholesale produce vendors, and stores selling caps, work shirts, and the cargo hooks used by longshoremen to lift bags of coffee, wheat, and rice. All the while you would have heard the sounds of winches, engines, foghorns, whistle blasts, and men shouting.

It was to this waterfront in early 1932 that Sam Darcy, the Communist Party's west-coast leader, brought several of his comrades to speak with longshoremen and sailors. "I attended many meetings on the waterfront at 7 o'clock in the morning, and sometimes addressed them," recalled Orrick Johns in his memoir *Time of Our Lives*.

> The men were rebellious against their working conditions, their pay and the black-listing "fink halls" to which they had to go to get employment—but at our Communist meetings they were often sullen and indifferent . . . Only after the longshoremen and marines found leaders among their own workers was it possible to organize them solidly.

They found their main leader in Harry Bridges, a left-wing Australian national who had been working as a San Francisco longshoreman for a decade. After seeing Darcy and his men on the docks, Bridges joined a small group of Party members and left-wing longshoremen at the end of 1932. Before long he was leading the effort to organize the waterfront.

Throughout the first half of 1933, Bridges and his fellow organizers talked to hundreds of longshoremen about building a rank-and-file union. But they made little progress until June of that year, when President Roosevelt's National Industrial Recovery Act promised workers the right to collective bargaining. Before then, businesses faced no legal consequences for disregarding unions. The new law gave workers the right to form unions that employers had to bargain with.

So the New York-based International Longshoremen's Association immediately granted a charter to a San Francisco longshoreman who requested it, in part, to counter the Communists and other left-wingers who had been trying to organize the waterfront. Bridges and his comrades had no choice but to accept the new union, encourage the men to join, and try to take charge of it.

Most longshoremen joined the union that summer, and Bridges got control of it by the fall. He was thin but wiry tough after ten years of hooking bales, lifting boxes, and operating the heavy steel levers of the loading winches. He liked to swear, dress shabbily, and go unshaven, perhaps to compensate for his middle-class background and parochial school education. His quick wits, enormous energy, and way with words made him a master—according to the authors of the 1937 book *Men Who Lead Labor*—at talking to longshoremen and listening to their complaints:

> He would nod his narrow head, a smile curving his thin lips, "Of course," he would snort. Workers on the waterfront learned to expect those two impatient words from Bridges, the cock-sure "of course" that invariably greeted their grumbling and preceded the angry explanation of how they could combat the employers . . . Like most longshoremen, Bridges enjoyed a drink and liked to hang around talking in the saloons along the water-front. He preached the same sermon endlessly, often arrogant in his certainty and impatient of those who had other ideas. But Bridges also had a sly humor that amused other workers, and an integrity that impressed them . . . One thing Bridges grasped—and repeated endlessly—that class was aligned against class, that workers and employers were ever opposed, and that their strug-gle could not be solved by compromise.

Every longshoreman who talked to Bridges knew he was left-wing. Most heard the rumors about his ties to Communists. Some guessed correctly that he wrote the *Waterfront Worker*, a local paper published anonymously by the Party until Sam Darcy gave it to Bridges, who continued to publish it without a byline. A few even thought Bridges was a member of the Communist Party. Bridges always denied it, but we now know that he did in fact join the Party:

Maynard Dixon, *Scab*, 1934, oil on canvas.

no later than 1935, almost certainly before. Regardless of when he joined, by the fall of 1933 he was already straddling the line between being an open leader of a fledgling labor union and a secret supporter of the Communist Party.

Late that fall, Bridges called for representatives of all west-coast longshoremen to meet in San Francisco in early 1934. At that February meeting, Bridges insisted on immediate negotiations with ship-owners while pushing the line "One port down, all down." The longshoremen of the several west-coast ports, in other words, would strike together to prevent ship-owners from playing off one port against another.

The ship-owners recognized the new union, but negotiations broke down after two months. The main sticking point was who controlled the hiring hall: that is, who decided who worked which jobs. The union wanted full control, the ship-owners wanted joint control. So the union called a strike on May 9. Pickets went up, strikers

Hoodlums attacking Chinese; detail of the Rincon Annex mural by Anton Refregier.

Art, Politics, and History

Art deco style and New Deal politics combine beautifully in the Rincon Annex Post Office at Mission and Spear Streets. The streamlined building features stone-relief friezes of dolphins, burnished steel doorways framed by black marble, and a sleek lobby painted with 27 mural panels by Anton Refregier, a Russian immigrant who worked on several New Deal murals before winning, in 1941, the commission to paint the big lobby of the new post office.

Mural painting, according to Refregier, should not be "banal, decorative embellishment," but rather a "meaningful, significant, powerful plastic statement based on the history and lives of the people." His 27 panels in Rincon Annex are nothing if not significant and powerful. For they illustrate the arc of San Francisco history—from Mission Dolores proselytizers and anti-Chinese rioters to the Big Strike of 1934 and the naval shipyards of the Second World War—and they do so with vibrant colors and a social realist style meant to highlight political oppression and vindicate class struggle.

Refregier's mural probably suited the politics of most San Franciscans, but the government paid for it, and his artistic freedom was thus subject to public accountability. So the Catholic Church, New Deal officials, labor unions, and veterans groups all forced Refregier to make small changes—from shrinking the belly of a fat friar preaching to gaunt Ohlone Indians at Mission Dolores to removing images of Communists in the Big Strike—during his several years of painting. A bigger threat came in 1953, when a Congressional subcommittee led by conservative Republicans, including one from northern California, sought to expunge the 240-ft (70-m) mural. The would-be censors were quickly stopped, however, by two other California congressmen and by the Bay Citizens' Committee to Protect the Rincon Annex Murals. Refregier's mural remains open to the public, and illustrates a time when government-sponsored art was all at once moralizing, important, and beautiful.

scuffled with police, and longshoremen thrashed some would-be strike-breakers. Within a week every west-coast port was shut down. A week later a hundred ships were at anchor in San Francisco Bay, the strike's lead port.

For five weeks the tension mounted as teamsters lost work, longshoremen lost wages, and businessmen lost income. With the city's newspapers and politicians calling for a settlement, the New York boss of the International Longshoremen's Association –which had chartered the west-coast locals—went to San Francisco to cut a deal with the ship-owners. But Bridges and his longshoremen were not going to let an outsider settle their strike. On June 17, Bridges led a mass meeting of longshoremen in the Civic Auditorium to vote on the New York boss Joe Ryan's proposed deal. Several thousand men booed Ryan off the platform when he tried to explain the deal that he'd made without consulting the rank and file. The men then rejected Ryan's deal by voice vote.

The next day Bridges was elected chairman of a new Joint Marine Strike Committee, which took over all aspects of the strike, including negotiations. The day after that he invited San Francisco mayor Angelo Rossi to the auditorium for another mass meeting of longshoremen. Rossi was a self-made man who supported labor unions and the New Deal, but blamed Bridges and the Communist Party for radicalizing the strike. Like Joe Ryan before him, Rossi was treated roughly by the longshoremen: two Party members called for a general strike right in front of him. The lines had hardened.

Two weeks later, the ship-owners tried to break the strike. For the first time in three decades, a San Francisco mayor let policemen protect strike-breakers. The immediate result was two days of street fighting, most of it along the waterfront south of the Ferry Building. Six hundred policemen carrying pistols, shotguns, and tear gas, and riding cars, horses, and motorcycles, fought several thousand strikers wielding bricks and railroad spikes. Dozens of policemen and hundreds of strikers were hurt. On the afternoon of July 5, policemen shot and killed two workers.

That evening, National Guard troops took over the waterfront, Joe Ryan complained from New York that Bridges and the

Communist Party were "in control of the San Francisco situation," and Roosevelt's secretary of labor, Frances Perkins, asked Bridges via telephone to end the strike. Instead of calling off the strike, Bridges called for a general strike of all San Francisco workers. He reiterated his call at the next day's meeting of the San Francisco Labor Council, the umbrella organization for the city's many unions. But the Council's moderate leaders put off a vote on a general strike in order to give the ship-owners and strikers a chance to agree to arbitration by Roosevelt's National Longshoremen's Board.

Bridges regained the momentum a few days later while riding in one of two cars that led a stunning funeral procession up Market Street for the murdered workers. Bridges rode with the mother of jailed labor radical Tom Mooney, who had been convicted—unjustly, as it turned out—for detonating a bomb that killed ten people during a San Francisco march for military preparedness in 1916. Local Communist Party leader Sam Darcy rode in the second car with the widow of the dead striker who was a Party member. Bridges and Darcy must have enjoyed the irony of their leading the funeral parade. For the chief of police had agreed to let Bridges's Strike Committee manage the procession so long as it kept the Communists out of the way.

The parade began at union headquarters near the corner of Steuart and Mission, just a block from the docks. As the parade started north towards Market Street, Bridges would have seen the first tower of the future Bay Bridge over his right shoulder. He knew that Roosevelt's New Deal was paying for it. He also knew that Roosevelt had codified the right to collective bargaining, which sparked the formation of the union whose strike he was leading. And he knew, as the parade turned onto Market Street and he caught a glimpse of Coit Tower, that New Deal money had paid for the interior murals that were delaying the opening of the white Art Deco spire. Three of the tower's two dozen muralists (Victor Arnautoff, Bernard Zakheim, and Clifford Wight) were in the Communist Party and had worked with Diego Rivera in Mexico. A number of other muralists had been influenced by Rivera's trip to San Francisco in 1931, when he painted murals in the California Stock Exchange and the California School

Longshoremen and policemen fighting amid tear gas, July 1934.

Two longshoremen killed by police on July 5, 1934.

Part of a mural in Coit Tower.

of Fine Arts. So it's no surprise that some of the murals in Coit Tower included images of a hammer and sickle, Karl Marx's *Das Kapital* and various Communist Party newspapers—images that proved controversial enough to prevent the tower from opening during the strike.

Roosevelt's influence was all over San Francisco: in the strike itself, in the Bay Bridge, in Coit Tower's murals, in Dorothea Lange's

Dorothea Lange, *Street Demonstration—San Francisco/The General Strike—Policeman*, 1934.

photos and in a dozen other New Deal projects employing thousands of workers. Yet Bridges was pushing beyond the politics of the New Deal by pushing the strike as far left as he could in a city willing to grant him considerable latitude. He'd spurned a request to end the strike from Roosevelt's secretary of labor, and now he was urging a general strike and advising his longshoremen to deny federal authorities the power to arbitrate the impasse.

As the parade advanced up Market Street, Bridges must have sensed its power—and the momentum it was giving him. "The procession was orderly and quiet," observed Paul Eliel, who did research for the ship-owners and wrote the first detailed account of the strike:

> Every marcher walked with head bared. Not a word was spoken. None smoked. The ranks were well formed and the cadence of the marchers' feet was set by the slow music of a Beethoven funeral march played by a single band . . . It was one of the strangest and most dramatic spectacles that had ever moved along Market Street. Its passage marked the high tide of united labor action in San Francisco . . . As the last marcher broke ranks, the certainty of a general strike, which up to this time had appeared to many to be the visionary dream of a small group of the most militant workers, became for the first time a practical and realizable objective.

A general strike became a practical objective because the funeral procession all at once brought the rest of the city's workers closer to the longshoremen, dissolved divisions among the longshoremen themselves about the wisdom of a general strike, and generated more sympathy among ordinary San Franciscans for the strikers and their cause.

Bridges used the power of the parade to resist calls for federal arbitration from fellow labor leaders and from the ship-owners themselves. At a mass meeting of the powerful Teamsters union, he convinced the Teamsters (and dozens of smaller unions) to strike in sympathy with his longshoremen. And a few days after that, on July 15, he convinced the San Francisco Labor Council to vote in favor of an immediate general strike.

The next day the city's economy came to a halt. Hardly any stores opened, hardly any factories operated, hardly anyone went to work. But Bridges quickly lost control of his general strike. The Labor Council's leaders made sure it remained a sympathy strike for economic gains instead of becoming a radical strike for political purposes.

Communist Party headquarters damaged during the general strike.

To that end, they rebuffed, ignored, and weakened controls that Bridges sought to place on businesses—controls that would have given the General Strike Committee the power to decide, for instance, who could operate their truck or open their store or restaurant. And on July 17, the second day of the general strike, Labor Council leaders passed a resolution asking west-coast mayors and governors to urge President Roosevelt to ask the strikers and ship-owners to let his National Longshoremen's Board arbitrate their dispute. Most San Franciscans supported the strikers, especially after the shootings and the funeral procession; but few were willing to countenance a protracted general strike that rejected arbitration by Roosevelt's National Longshoremen's Board.

Two days later, the Labor Council's leaders passed a resolution calling for the longshoremen and sailors to submit to arbitration and end their strike. The Teamsters voted immediately to return to work. The longshoremen then agreed to take a vote on arbitration. Bridges pleaded with them to vote against it, but they voted for it and returned to work. Abandoned by the Teamsters and long-shoremen, the sailors went back to their ships. The ship-owners, meanwhile, reiterated their earlier offer to arbitrate unconditionally with the longshoremen and bargain collectively with the sailors. The general strike was over in four days. Three months later, Roosevelt's National Longshoremen's Board gave the longshoremen everything they wanted.

Apart from his friends in the Communist Party, nobody wanted Bridges to prolong or radicalize the general strike. Yet his longshoremen, along with most blue-collar workers and plenty of other San Franciscans as well, were happy to let him take it a good long way. The intransigence of the ship-owners, the police protection given to strike-breakers, the murder of two strikers, the dramatic funeral procession, the politics of the New Deal, the unorthodox character of San Francisco—all helped turn a waterfront strike into a political battle that went as far to the left as things ever go in the United States.

Over the next three years Bridges built a powerful new union called the International Longshore and Warehouse Union—while he was secretly a member of the Central Committee of the Communist Party USA. Several years later, Bridges and the Big Strike were commemorated in a panel on a large New Deal mural (in the Rincon Annex Post Office) depicting the sweep of San Francisco history. Nobody knows how long Bridges stayed in the Party, but for the next forty years he kept his secret, ran his union, served on the Port Commission and enjoyed his status as a political celebrity.

Cocktails and a car in downtown, *c.* 1955.

5 Baghdad-by-the-Bay

In 1949 San Francisco's great newspaper columnist Herb Caen said, "It's nice to be part of a city that is proud of itself, a city that carries itself straight and tall on the slopes of its hills, the better to gaze fondly over its own charms." Caen always checked his keen enthusiasm for San Francisco with a quip—in this case about the city's high opinion of itself. Like most San Franciscans, however, Caen sincerely enjoyed living in a good-looking city with strong labor unions and a big appetite for pleasure. And he took great pride from living in a city he saw as

> truly "cosmopolitan"—that is, remarkably free from condescension, chauvinism, and petty friction. I like the daily sight of Negroes working at self-respecting jobs for the municipal government, running streetcars, handling the grips on a cable car, driving buses. I salute the new superintendent of education for promptly appointing a Negro as principal of a large school.

Caen made note of black San Franciscans because they grew in number during the 1940s from less than 5,000 to more than 40,000. They settled chiefly in the Fillmore district, which had been the main Jewish neighborhood for half a century and was home, as well, to a few thousand Japanese. "Only in Fillmore's 'Little Harlem'," Caen wrote, "are the sidewalks teeming with people in their Sunday best and worst, lounging, talking, standing in busy knots." But Caen knew that the sidewalks were teeming, in part, because people needed to escape their cramped apartments: "a tenement is bad enough during the week," he wrote, "but on a sunny Sunday it is unbearable." Another 30,000 blacks moved to San Francisco during the 1950s.

While many of them settled in the southeastern Bayview district, "the center of Negro life continues to be Fillmore Street, which despite its tawdry aspects," according to Harold Gilliam, in *The Face of San Francisco*, "is full of verve and spirit—brilliant flashing signs, jazzed-up store fronts, blaring juke boxes. Fillmore's night-time crowds are larger than those of any other neighborhood in the city."

The Fillmore was like a small black metropolis. It had all manner of churches, every class of people, and the best jazz scene outside of New York City. Doctors, maids, teachers, and day laborers lived on the same blocks and shopped at the same stores. Rich and poor lived side by side because black people, even wealthy black people, couldn't easily move to other neighborhoods. (The seller of a house that Willie Mays wanted to buy, for example, refused to sell until Mayor George Christopher publicly shamed him by inviting Mays to stay at his home.) Only the churches, according to *The Face of San Francisco*, "even begin to bridge the gulf dividing the Negro community between the educated and the uneducated. Outside the churches, the two groups find little in common socially." The Fillmore's *Sun Reporter* similarly lamented the wide gaps in education, wealth, and behavior among the neighborhood's people, and it complained about the discrimination they faced in job and housing markets. In general, though, the black weekly was optimistic about the progress of its people. The paper touted the hiring of San Francisco's first black fireman, city clerk, assistant district attorney, and housing-authority commissioner. And it reflected the view of its readers that they were far better off in San Francisco than they had been in Texas or Louisiana.

Caen gave another example of what he saw as the city's remarkable freedom from condescension and chauvinism. "In only a few years," he wrote, "as these things are reckoned, the Chinese and Japanese have become integral parts of the civic scenery—in almost every kind of job and profession in almost every part of the city." Caen was thinking about the 3,000 persons of Japanese descent whom federal authorities took from their homes in 1941 and put in internment camps throughout the war—yet who had, for the most part, regained their jobs and places in the city. And he was thinking about the much larger Chinese community. In 1938 Caen saw 100,000 visitors attend a "Chinatown Night" sponsored by the *San Francisco Chronicle*. After China sided with America in the Second World War, he saw Congress repeal the Chinese Exclusion Act. During the second half of the 1940s, he saw the number of Chinese in San Francisco grow by 50 percent, the first Chinese American get a municipal job, and thousands leave Chinatown for better parts of San Francisco.

All of that inspired Caen to call San Francisco "Baghdad-by-the-Bay": an exotic and beautiful crossroads where all kinds of people get

Young Japanese American going to an internment camp, 1941.

The caption for this *San Francisco Chronicle* photo reads "No one along Skid Road is likely to shop carefully," 1956.

along—or at least leave each other alone. Caen was smart, observant, and realistic, and he knew the city as well as anyone. So he knew that a number of white San Franciscans felt superior to blacks, Chinese, and Mexicans. He knew that the city had some bad cops and corrupt officials. He knew that capitalists and workers often clashed. He knew about the Fillmore's overcrowded buildings. He knew, as well, that St Anthony's fed 1,000 hungry people each day in the Tenderloin. Yet Caen believed the city deserved to be proud of itself. For San Francisco in the 1940s and '50s had as many types of people, and as little poverty, racial hatred, and ethnic chauvinism, as any city in the world. And it offered more opportunities for more of its people than ever before.

The Second World War effectively ended the Depression in San Francisco by making the Bay Area the Pacific theater's premier command and supply center. More than a million soldiers and sailors passed through the city, filling its hotels, restaurants, and bars. Hundreds of regional businesses supplied everything from boats and guns to boots, uniforms, and food rations. Airbases and naval yards serviced and supplied planes and ships. People from all over the country came to work in Bay Area factories. San Francisco alone gained 140,000 people during the 1940s. And right through the 1950s it remained the headquarters of major rail and shipping lines, of big banks like Wells Fargo and Bank of America, of mighty companies like Folgers, Levi Strauss, Bechtel, PG&E, Crown Zellerbach, and Standard Oil of California. The city also housed a Federal Reserve bank, a U.S. Mint, a branch of the Army Corps of Engineers, the naval shipyard at Hunters Point, and the state's Supreme Court and Public Utilities Commission. In 1958 San Francisco lured the Giants baseball team from New York, a coup celebrated with one of the biggest parades in city history.

While blacks were settling into the Fillmore and Bayview, and Chinese Americans were moving to the Richmond and Sunset districts, most whites (with the exception of young couples moving to new homes in the suburbs) stayed in their neighborhoods. By the late 1940s a typical family in a white neighborhood had siblings and cousins a block or two away, and had known its shopkeepers and neighbors for many years. Nearly all elementary- and middle-school kids walked to school and played on stoops and sidewalks. Women and teenagers didn't enjoy the freedoms they later would, but their neighborhoods were safe and comfortable, and their husbands and fathers were making good money in America's most unionized city. The average wage grew by more than 50 percent (in real terms) between the end of the war and the end of the 1950s.

Life is never altogether fair or good, but the vast majority of San Franciscans thought it was getting better. There is no doubt, for example, that wealth was more evenly distributed during the 1940s

View from the Mark Hopkins Hotel, *c.* 1950.

and '50s than ever before—or since. And even though white men generally had greater freedoms and more opportunities than blacks, Asians, Mexicans, and white women, sociologist Earl Raab captured the overall sense of fairness with this comment about Jews in 1950: "There are 55,000 Jews in San Francisco," he wrote in *There's No City Like San Francisco*,

> and not even the historic traces of a ghetto. There is a Jewish community that has been called, with reason, the wealthiest, per capita, in the country. There is at the same time a startling poverty of anti-Semitic tradition. So far as the city and its institutions are concerned, the Jew is a first-class citizen. It may well be that he can live in San Francisco with a greater degree of personal dignity than in any other large city in the country.

If San Francisco in the mid-1950s was richer, freer, and fairer than ever before, so too was it a nicer-looking city. Downtown's Art Deco skyscrapers were visible from many parts of the city, yet the tallest was only 32 stories. So they didn't block views of the city or tower over it. And they were well proportioned, smartly decorated and made from brick, stone, and terracotta. From their upper floors you would have seen a busy waterfront, nicely dressed people on crowded sidewalks, and trolleys and cable cars sharing the streets with the best-looking automobiles ever made. No part of the city had been defiled by elevated freeways, pocked by empty factories and warehouses, or demolished by the wrecking ball of redevelopment. To look south, west, and north from a tall downtown building was to enjoy a clear view of the soft-looking hills, and the light-colored buildings, that had inspired Edmund Wilson a decade before to call San Francisco the Camembert City.

Even good times have bad features, and a major failing of the late 1940s and '50s was its fierce Americanization. The Cold War, economic prosperity, and a mood of political acquiescence spurred Congress to put "In God We Trust" on the currency and allowed Senator Joseph McCarthy to harass left-wingers. More than any other place, however, San Francisco left alone its atheists, oddballs, leftists, libertines, and homosexuals. And it had proportionately more of them than any other American city. So it was easy for Mayor George Christopher to invite Nikita Khrushchev to San Francisco in 1959. The Soviet premier so enjoyed his warm reception—which included a visit to Harry Bridges at his union headquarters—that he invited the mayor to visit the USSR. The mayor went.

It's no wonder, then, that San Francisco was ready for the Beat rebellion before the rest of the country. "But we couldn't have pulled it off alone," recalled poet and printer William Everson in *San Francisco Beat: Talking with the Poets*: "It took something outside ourselves . . . As it turned out, Allen Ginsberg and Jack Kerouac provided the ingredients. They came to San Francisco and found themselves, and it was *their* finding that sparked us."

Ginsberg found himself in "Howl," which he first read publicly in San Francisco in 1955. Its opening lines are probably the best he ever wrote, and they sparked artists like Everson:

> I saw the best minds of my generation destroyed by madness,
>   starving hysterical naked,
> dragging themselves through the negro streets at dawn looking
>   for an angry fix,
> angelheaded hipsters burning for the ancient heavenly
>   connection to the starry dynamo in the machinery of night . . .

Kerouac found himself in *On the Road*, whose manic intensity was inspired, he wrote in *Esquire*, by a "vision" he'd had

> of a generation of crazy, illuminated hipsters suddenly rising
> and roaming America, serious, curious, bumming and hitchhik-
> ing everywhere, ragged, beatific, beautiful in an ugly graceful
> new way—a vision gleaned from the way we had heard the word
> *beat* spoken on streetcorners on Times Square and in the
> Village, in other cities in the downtown-city-night of post-
> war America—*beat*, meaning down and out but full of intense
> conviction.

Herb Caen at his desk, 1953.

Mr. San Francisco

Others may have loved their cities as much as Herb Caen loved San Francisco, but no one else wrote a daily newspaper column about their city for six decades. Caen's columns were often about his many friends—from William Saroyan and Harry Bridges in the 1940s and '50s to Willie Brown and Robin Williams in the 1980s and '90s. And he was famous for coining epithets like "Beatniks" and "Berserkeley." But Caen also broke news stories and wrote shrewdly about the city's politics and culture.

Caen and San Francisco were made for each other. They both liked personal freedom, backed labor unions, and thought highly of themselves. Like so many San Franciscans, Caen came to the city as a young person (in 1936) from somewhere else (Sacramento) and as something of an outsider (he was Jewish). And he was a walker in a city full of spectacular views, interesting people, and a wide variety of bars, clubs, and restaurants. Caen wrote in the morning, took long lunches with a couple of dry martinis, returned to his office to answer letters, and spent his evenings at dinner parties and society events. He always wore a suit and fedora.

Herb Caen saw the bridges get built. He watched the rise of beats, hippies, and homosexuals. He complained about modern skyscrapers and he witnessed the first dot-com boom. "Nothing is what it used to be," he said in the early 1990s. "That doesn't mean it is worse, though . . . I am not bitter about the way The City is going. I am just confused, mainly, and I find it very hard to write about now because I can't quite see The City the way I could see it once." Even if Caen did believe that San Francisco was better in the 1940s and '50s, he never stopped loving it or trying to understand it—which is why he won a special Pulitzer Prize in 1996 for "extraordinary and continuing contribution as a voice and conscience of his city." It seems fitting that he won the prize while turning eighty and marrying his fourth wife.

If Kerouac's idea of Beat combined upbeat, downbeat, and deadbeat, Ginsberg's was being "wide-eyed" and, like Walt Whitman, "receptive to a vision"—a vision of extreme personal liberty mixed with spiritual empathy for others.

Their idea of Beat also meant giving the finger to society at large. Ginsberg was sensitive, Jewish, and gay. He literally had visions of the great romantic William Blake, whom he mentions in "Howl." And he complained (in his essay "Poetry, Violence, and the Trembling Lambs") about a "sexless and soulless America" with a "false image of its Authority" and a "mechanical consciousness" that represses "deviants from the mass sexual stereotype." If his complaints were general, his politics were personal: "individual acts of mercy." Kerouac, on the other hand, was tough, Catholic, and working class. He was not critical of America in a political sense—he voted for Eisenhower—but he and the characters in his books were always fleeing the square everyday stuff of manners, relationships, and responsibilities. Neither Kerouac nor his characters stopped for very long in any place, or for anybody or anything. Instead, they frenetically devoured experience after experience, all of them off the American mainstream and along the alternate channels of back roads, skid rows, rail yards, vice districts, bohemian quarters, and bebop clubs. "Sal, we gotta go and never stop going till we get there," says Dean Moriarty in *On the Road*. "Where we going, man?" "I don't know but we gotta go."

Ginsberg wrote an arresting and timely poem. And even though Kerouac's high-speed prose—he called it "spontaneous bop prosody"—caused Truman Capote to quip "that's not writing, that's just typewriting," Kerouac created a new and exciting attitude. In fact, creating attitude was the true genius of Kerouac and Ginsberg. The attitude combined the idea of pure rebellion—against society in general but nothing in particular—with an inspired search for personal freedom to be sought on the road, in nature, among black jazz musicians, by becoming one with Zen, and through sex and drugs.

The attitude found a home in San Francisco. In an interview with the *Examiner* in October 1958, Kerouac said "San Francisco was the last great city in America ... my mad, wild playtown." Kerouac, Ginsberg, and other Beat writers like Gregory Corso, Philip Whalen,

Michael McClure, and Lawrence Ferlinghetti had all moved to San Francisco by the early 1950s. "Who cares about geography?" asked Kerouac. "San Francisco is the poetry center of America today." Kerouac was half right: the home geographies of the poets didn't matter, but the geography of San Francisco did. For it was the city itself that attracted the Beats, and nurtured them while they were there.

Lawrence Ferlinghetti wrote poems and owned City Lights bookstore, which published Ginsberg's "Howl." Half a century later, during his inaugural address as the city's first poet laureate, he recalled coming to San Francisco:

> When I arrived in the City in 1950, I came overland by train and took the ferry from the Oakland mole to the Ferry Building. And San Francisco looked like some Mediterranean port—a small white city, with mostly white buildings—a little like Tunis seen from seaward. I thought perhaps it was Atlantis, risen from the sea.

Writer Kenneth Rexroth arrived two decades before Ferlinghetti. In his introduction to the 1957 edition of the *Evergreen Review*, which featured San Francisco's Beat poets, Rexroth wrote:

> It is easy to understand why all this has centered in San Francisco. It is a long way from Astor Place or Kenyon College. It is one of the easiest cities in the world to live in. It is the easiest in America. Its culture is genuinely . . . Mediterranean—*laissez faire* and *dolce far niente*.

The Beats benefited from Rexroth's central position in the Bay Area literary scene. For years he'd been holding open houses for local poets. In 1954 he founded the Poetry Center at San Francisco State College and invited W. H. Auden to its opening. A year later he was master of ceremonies at the Six Gallery when Ginsberg first read "Howl." Here is how Ginsberg recounted the event two years later in his essay "The Six Gallery Reading":

A group of six unknown poets in San Francisco, in a moment of drunken enthusiasm, decided to defy the system of academic poetry, official reviews, New York publishing machinery, national sobriety and generally accepted good standards of taste, by giving a free reading of their poetry in a run down second rate experimental art gallery in the Negro section of San Francisco.

The gallery was not so run down. Nor was it in the black section of town. But Ginsberg accurately conveyed the jubilantly rebellious attitude of the "six unknown poets"—five of whom read while Kerouac drunkenly urged them on.

If the Beats were enticed by San Francisco's easy living, inveterate bohemianism, and Mediterranean beauty, they were especially charmed by North Beach, an Italian neighborhood close to downtown, Chinatown, and the old Barbary Coast. North Beach had plenty of cheap restaurants, and its long-time residents didn't seem to mind having several hundred Beats in their midst. Because bohemians had been living on the south side of North Beach for decades, there were a number of tiny cafés with guttering candles in empty claret bottles, and several well-known hang-outs like Vesuvio, Black Cat Café, and The Cellar, which hosted the first readings of poetry to live jazz. The century-old Montgomery Block building housed dozens of artist studios, and the California School of Fine Arts was only a few blocks up the hill from Columbus Avenue, the neighborhood's main drag. Painters Clyfford Still, Richard Diebenkorn, and Mark Rothko, along with photographers Ansel Adams, Dorothea Lange, Lisette Model, and Imogen Cunningham, all studied or taught at the school during the late 1940s and '50s. And by 1953 North Beach had Ferlinghetti's City Lights bookstore. Ferlinghetti loved North Beach, which he saw for the first time in 1950. He realized at once that it was "a poetic place, as poetic as some quartiers in Paris, as any place in old Europa, as poetic as any place great poets and painters had found inspiration."

The Beats hit their peak—in North Beach, in San Francisco, and as a social and artistic movement—in 1956, '57 and '58. Ferlinghetti's

City Lights published "Howl" in 1956. The next year, Ginsberg and City Lights won an obscenity trial aimed at the poem's homosexual passages. The trial got national attention. That same year Kerouac's *On the Road* came out. The book was widely reviewed. By then the Beats had created a vibrant scene in the bars, cafés, and restaurants of North Beach. People read aloud their own poems, and they read aloud passages from Henry Miller's *Tropic of Cancer* and D. H. Lawrence's *Lady Chatterley's Lover*, which were banned. The men started wearing goatees and berets, the women capri pants and straight hair. Groups of self-identifying Beats marched downtown—as Beats—to display themselves to ordinary San Franciscans. National magazines and city newspapers sent reporters to San Francisco to write stories about Beat poets and their Beat life.

Herb Caen liked having the Beats in his Baghdad-by-the-Bay. By 1958, however, the Beat scene had become, well, a scene. So Caen

City Lights bookstore, *c.* 1958.

made fun of the poets, the wannabe poets, and the many hangers-on, by calling them "beatniks." (He was punning off the word "sputnik.") In 1995 he told a *Chronicle* reporter about the first time he used the term in his newspaper column: "I ran into Kerouac that night at El Matador. He was mad. He said, 'You're putting us down and making us sound like jerks. I hate it. Stop using it.'" Caen said he

made fun of the beats because they took themselves so seriously. Ginsberg was all right. I had a drink with him one night at Vesuvio and we walked across the street to the Tosca. He was barefoot. The uptight Italian who owned the place kicked him

Man reading from *Lady Chatterley's Lover* in North Beach, c. 1958.

Vesuvio's owner in front of an "ad" for Beatnik Kit.

out. "But I'm Allen Ginsberg!" he shouted. The guy had never heard of him.

But the Beats had a laugh on Caen. Someone put up a poster in the Co-existence Bagel Shop, a Beat hangout, that said, "We feature separate toilet facilities for HERB CAEN."

March to end employment discrimination in front of a Cadillac showroom, 1964.

6 Lefties, Gays, and Hippies

That San Francisco had seen better days became obvious to me while riding as a bike messenger for six months in 1978 and 1979. Vacant lots pocked lower Market Street. The double-deck Embarcadero freeway walled off the city from its bay. One of the Ferry Building's few remaining tenants was a bike messenger company. The financial district employed tens of thousands of white-collar workers, but hardly any of them stayed after work to eat, drink, or watch a movie. And if twenty new office towers signaled downtown's continued dominance as a business center, their rectilinear forms and glass walls looked cold and anonymous next to older skyscrapers with step-back profiles clothed in Deco- and Gothic-styled masonry.

Other parts of the city were also past their primes. I rode by abandoned piers to pick up packages from a printing press in a run-down warehouse zone south of Market Street. I lived in Haight-Ashbury, where a quarter of all storefronts were boarded up and nearby Golden Gate Park was a mess. I liked going to the Mission District on Saturdays to eat tacos and watch the line of exquisitely painted low-riders bounce along Mission Street, but the stores were shabby and many of the neighborhood's Victorians needed repairs. While walking one day through the mostly black Western Addition, I came upon a dozen square blocks of empty space: an entire section of the neighborhood had been obliterated.

It was easy to see that the city had once been better, but I had no idea that San Francisco had been in physical and economic decline for two decades. During those years the waterfront lost its ships and longshoremen to a new container port in Oakland. Hundreds of manufacturers went out of business and laid off 15,000 workers. Dozens of Art Deco movie theaters shut their doors. The Tenderloin devolved into a central-city slum full of porno shops, street hustlers, drug peddlers, prostitutes, and low-end stores. San Francisco's population declined by almost 10 percent, and would have fallen further if not for 80,000 immigrants from China and Central America. All the while tax revenues fell while crime rates rose. No wonder Herb Caen worried about "our little world of a city-state falling apart."

Nor did I understand that redevelopment had created the huge empty space I saw in the Western Addition. San Francisco used federal money in the late 1950s and '60s to buy up and tear down more than 2,000 century-old Victorians. Various forms of public housing replaced some of the demolished buildings, but more than a dozen blocks remained vacant for decades. Most of the people forced out by redevelopment were black. They moved to Bayview-Hunter's Point, to the northeast corner of Haight-Ashbury, and to the Tenderloin. Whereas Caen saw hope and progress for blacks in the 1940s and '50s, by 1965 he knew that "The 'Negro' problem is very much with the city, too." By then Fillmore Street was run-down, most of its jazz clubs had closed and the wrecking ball of redevelopment was in full swing. A year later, people in Bayview-Hunter's Point took to the streets in a small-scale riot to protest the killing of an unarmed young man by a police officer. City hall immediately sent in social workers and started community programs. They didn't solve the underlying problems, but they probably helped prevent more rioting—and helped prevent the opening of a San Francisco chapter of Oakland's Black Panther Party.

San Francisco would have been much worse off—and far less fascinating—if not for three social movements that distinguished it from every other American city in the 1960s and '70s. The first movement democratized the process of redevelopment in the city. The hulking Embarcadero freeway opened in 1959. It was supposed to be the first section of 25 miles (40 km) of San Francisco freeways built by the state highway commission. But merchants and homeowners in the paths of several proposed freeways—which were slated to run along the entire Embarcadero, through the Marina and across Golden Gate Park—protested their construction. So did several politicians, the *San Francisco Chronicle*, and a small group of activists. Together they stalled construction with years of hearings, and eventually killed the very idea of building more freeways in San Francisco. The city took over highway planning from the state, and the Board of Supervisors passed a resolution stating that new transit projects must enhance "land values, human values, and the preservation of the city's treasured appearance." National magazines called it "the San Francisco freeway revolt."

Stopping the freeways was the first step in a gradual shift of power from downtown business interests to neighborhood groups and community activists. Though these new groups and activists sometimes worked at cross-purposes, they were all liberals and leftists trying to influence the direction of the city. To that end, they lobbied sympathetic supervisors, organized street protests, waged legal battles, sponsored ballot initiatives, and spoke up at meetings of the Planning Commission and Board of Supervisors. By the

Downtown redevelopment project near the Embarcadero freeway, 1963.

late 1960s they had forced the city to provide housing for people displaced by redevelopment, and they had secured the right for neighborhoods to participate in redevelopment plans. By the end of the 1970s they had made rent control a law, put height limits on new apartment buildings, and banned the demolition of single-room occupancy hotels, which house poor people. A few years later they sponsored a successful ballot initiative to cap annual office construction in the financial district. By the mid-1980s, San Francisco had the country's strictest growth controls and its thickest web of community organizations.

While left-wing activists and neighborhood groups fought for political power, homosexuals were fighting for personal liberties—liberties they had begun to secure by the time I got to San Francisco in 1978. Soon after arriving, I found Armistead Maupin's *Tales of the City* in a laundromat on Haight Street. The new book had been first published in serial form in the *San Francisco Chronicle*. It featured homosexuals cruising bars, gay people at risk of blackmail, and married men meeting other men in bathhouses. Its charming protagonist, Anna Madrigal, was formerly a man. During a conversation with a

The financial district, 1975.

Mock street signs in the Castro, 1975.

straight young woman about the many gay men (some 70,000) living in San Francisco, Madrigal tells her: "Take it as a challenge. When a woman triumphs in this town she *really* triumphs."

Reading *Tales of the City* made me want to visit the Castro, the world's first explicitly gay neighborhood. It seemed like a world apart. For the Castro was inhabited mainly by men, nearly all of them homosexual. Most of its stores, bars, gyms, restaurants, and sex shops had no female customers or workers. The entire place was thick with male energy. The Castro was not only America's first *gay* neighborhood: it was also its first *gentrified* neighborhood. By the mid-1960s, middle-class gay men from across the country were replacing the Castro's working-class population. And they were renovating and redecorating the neighborhood's ornate houses. Richard Rodriguez called them "dollhouses for libertines" in his cheeky essay "Late Victorians."

San Francisco had always been relatively open to people with alternative sexual tastes, but the prospect of a specifically homosexual neighborhood probably arose during the Second World War. Thousands of gay soldiers who had disembarked for war from San Francisco, or were discharged from war in San Francisco, decided to live there. By the mid-1950s there were at least a dozen gay bars, mostly on Polk Street and in the Tenderloin, and there were gay rights groups like the Mattachine Society and Daughters of Bilitis. By the time *Life* magazine named San Francisco the "Gay Capital of the U.S." in 1964, the Society for Individual Rights was sponsoring everything from bridge clubs to drag clubs while pressing politicians to stop the police from harassing gays. In 1966 the Society established the nation's first gay and lesbian community center. That same year some twenty or thirty drag queens hanging around Compton's Cafeteria in the Tenderloin brawled with policemen who had been called to clear them out. This small riot over sexual identity happened three years before New York City's Stonewall riots.

Despite sporadic police raids on gay bars and periodic arrests of gay men in parks, homosexuals were gaining acceptance in the city and turning the Castro into their own neighborhood. Gay men held a Drag Ball in a major hotel in 1969. A gay section of Polk

Gay men at a Halloween street party in the Castro, *c.* 1975.

Gay protest march with images of Stalin, Hitler, Mugabe, the KKK, and Anita Bryant, 1977.

Street threw a wild Halloween street party in 1970. The first gay pride parade marched down Polk Street to city hall in 1972. Later that year, gay activists convinced the Board of Supervisors to prohibit city contractors from discriminating against homosexuals.

The time had come for gay people to stop relying on straight but sympathetic liberals, and for someone to run openly as a gay politician. That person was Harvey Milk. Because Milk had no political experience and was mistrusted by long-time gay leaders, who saw him as a brash interloper, he badly lost his first run for supervisor in 1973. But Milk was shrewd, outgoing, and ambitious. He organized the first Castro Street Fair and styled himself the "Mayor of Castro Street." After losing a second run for supervisor in 1975, he mastered the art of getting himself in the newspapers and making alliances with anyone who'd help his cause. With endorsements from the *Chronicle* and the *Examiner,* and the votes of almost everyone in the Castro, Milk finally won a supervisor's seat in November 1977. As the country's first openly gay city official, he immediately sponsored an ordinance that would help homosexuals "come out" by barring discrimination against them in hiring, housing, and public accommodations.

Milk's ordinance was supported by liberal mayor George Moscone, whose election in 1975 marked what the *Examiner* called "a turning point between the old 'ins' and the newly awakened neighborhood 'outs.'" Liberals won the city's top elected posts—mayor, sheriff, and district attorney—and Moscone appointed liberals and minorities to city commissions and departments. Just as neighborhood activists were gaining power at the expense of downtown business interests, so too were gay people gaining the power and support they would need to win full rights for themselves as American citizens. Soon after taking office, Moscone declared his intent to wipe away prejudice against homosexuals. "I will only be satisfied," he said, "if I can not only change the face of San Francisco, but change the soul of San Francisco, and, with its extraordinary international authority, become a catalyst for conversion for the rest of the country, if not the world."

With Moscone's backing, Milk's ordinance was passed by the Board of Supervisors in the spring of 1978. Only Dan White voted against it. That fall, White shot Milk and Moscone from point-blank range in City Hall. Board President (and future Mayor and Senator) Dianne Feinstein heard the shots, found Milk's body, and identified Moscone's corpse for the police. A little while later she was standing in front of the cameras. With a far-off look in her eyes she said, "As President of the Board it's my duty to make this announcement. Both Mayor Moscone and Supervisor Harvey Milk have been shot and killed. The suspect is Supervisor Dan White." The day after the shootings, the *New York Times* rightly noted that White had "made it clear that he saw himself as the board's defender of the home, the family and religious life against homosexuals, pot smokers and cynics." White murdered two progressive individuals, but he couldn't kill the expansion of personal liberties they stood for.

If progressives and gays redefined San Francisco in the 1960s and '70s, nothing defined the "sixties" better than Haight-Ashbury. In September 1965 Michael Fallon wrote four articles for the *Examiner* about a new bohemian quarter filling up with lesbians, homosexuals, pot smokers, artists, writers, musicians, crusaders for various causes, and people doing almost nothing at all. Fallon was probably the first writer to use the word "hippie" in its modern sense. Haight-Ashbury, he wrote, was fast becoming a place for "the outer fringe of the bohemian fringe—the 'hippies,' the 'heads,' the beatniks."

Drummers on Hippie Hill in Haight-Ashbury.

This outer fringe of San Francisco's bohemia would soon be at the center of American culture.

Music was to hippies what poetry was to Beats. By late 1965 impresario Bill Graham was organizing dance concerts in the Fillmore Auditorium. Graham made sure the shows started on time, were safe, and made money. "We were hippies," said David Freiberg of the band Quicksilver Messenger Service, "and we were pissed off at him for being a businessman. That is, until we got paid." The shows were packed with white middle-class kids dancing free-form to the early sounds of Quicksilver, Jefferson Airplane, the Grateful Dead, and Janis Joplin.

Topless at the Condor, *c.* 1970.

Erotic City

San Francisco's gold rush, Barbary Coast, and inveterate bohemianism primed it for launching modern American pornography in 1964, when Carol Doda took off her pasties and danced utterly topless at the Condor Club in North Beach. Within a year, two municipal judges had acquitted topless dancers of violating obscenity laws, three dozen clubs were featuring topless acts, and nine downtown stores openly sold pornography. By the late 1960s, when the California Supreme Court ruled pornography a protected form of speech, San Francisco's topless shows had become all-nude shows and the Mitchell Brothers were hosting lap dancing at the O'Farrell Theater. Gonzo journalist Hunter S. Thompson called the theater "the Carnegie Hall of public sex in America."

The *New York Times Magazine* was perfectly justified in calling San Francisco "The Porn Capital of America" in 1971. After describing its strip clubs, peep shows, and pornographic movie theaters, the article concluded that "walking around the city can give the casual visitor the impression that porn, not tourism, is San Francisco's leading industry." The business of porn grew even faster during the 1970s.

So did the twin business of selling sex. And in true San Francisco style, the liberal administration of Mayor George Moscone sought to decriminalize prostitution and curb the police corruption that went with it. To that end he appointed a broad-minded chief of police, Charles Gain, who became friends with Margo St James, a hooker whose day job was fighting for the rights of prostitutes. Chief Gain even attended Miss St James's annual Hookers' Ball in 1977. With all of its pornography and prostitution, and so many gay sex clubs and bathhouses, and a general tolerance for self-expression, San Francisco was surely a candidate for the world's most erotic city.

What made the new music scene truly special, however, was LSD. Ken Kesey was ten years older than most hippies and ten years younger than most Beats. He loved Kerouac's *On the Road* and did his own version of road-tripping—while on LSD with his Merry Pranksters in a colorfully painted school bus driven by Neal Cassady, Kerouac's former sidekick. In *The Electric Kool-aid Acid Test*, Tom Wolfe described the feeling of illumination shared by Kesey and his fellow trippers: "The world was simply and sheerly divided into 'the aware', those who had had the experience of being vessels of the divine, and a great mass of 'the unaware,' 'the unmusical,' 'the unattuned.' Or: *you're either on the bus or off the bus.*"

To get more people *on the bus*, Kesey organized a series of "acid tests" in late 1965. Groups of people took LSD, watched light shows, and listened to music, some of it by Jerry Garcia. The first tests took place at Kesey's country retreat just south of San Francisco; most of the rest were in the city. They culminated in a three-day Trips Festival in January 1966 at the Longshoremen's Hall near Fisherman's Wharf. After drinking punch laced with acid, several thousand people watched light shows and heard the Dead, the Airplane and Janis Joplin. Many of them dressed in the emerging costume of Haight-Ashbury: beads, beards, and long hair; boots, sandals, and moccasins; wide belts, tight blue jeans, and colorful corduroys; vests, paisley shirts, and granny dresses.

The Trips Festival was a hothouse version of what Haight-Ashbury would become over the next eighteen months. At the time of the festival, a few hundred "hippies" and "heads" were living in the declining middle-class neighborhood. For almost nothing you could rent an entire floor of a big Victorian loaded with scrollwork, stained glass, and bay windows. And you could meet kindred spirits on Haight Street, walk to Golden Gate Park and basically do as you pleased.

By spring of that year, Haight-Ashbury was gaining a reputation. After a big drug bust in the neighborhood, a police captain told the newspapers that "the word is out that San Francisco is the place for the far-out crowd." That summer the number of resident hippies reached a few thousand. Merchants on Haight Street responded to their needs: the Psychedelic Shop sold books, LSD, and drug paraphernalia; Mnasidika sold hippie clothing; the Print Mint sold posters for thumb-tacking on apartment walls. And the Grateful Dead, Jefferson Airplane, Quicksilver, and Janis Joplin lived in the neighborhood, played weekends at the Fillmore and the Avalon Ballroom, and sometimes performed for free on Haight Street and in Golden Gate Park.

Victor Moscoso made psychedelic posters to advertise the concerts. Years later he said 1966 was "when it worked. You'd walk down Haight and nod to another longhair and it *meant* something." He didn't say *what* it meant, but the scene was small and unique enough to create a special feeling of belonging—of being *on the bus*. Grateful Dead guitarist Bob Weir told *Rolling Stone* magazine that

> the folks who lived in our youth ghetto in Haight-Ashbury in '65 and '66 were of an artistic bent, almost all of them. Everyone brought something to the party. By the time of the Be-In people were coming just to be at the party, not bringing anything. I could see the whole thing tilting.

Just as the crashers began to arrive, the party announced itself to the world in a celebratory gathering called the Human Be-In. Nearly 20,000 people came together at the Polo Field in Golden Gate Park on January 14, 1967. They flew banners with an image of a pot leaf. They wore beads and buttons with messages of peace. They brought flowers, incense, and tambourines. And they smoked pot and dropped tabs of acid handed out by Owsley Stanley, the Grateful Dead's sound man and master craftsman of LSD. Beat poet Gary Snyder started off the gathering by blowing on a conch shell. Allen Ginsberg chanted "om." Timothy Leary told everyone to "Turn on, tune in, drop out." And the Dead, the Airplane and Quicksilver played their music. The Airplane's Paul Kantner saw a day filled with acid, incense, and balloons. At some point in the festivities, the impish Ginsberg looked out at the crowd, turned to Lawrence Ferlinghetti, and said, "What if we're wrong?"

Ginsberg was probably kidding, but he might have been clairvoyant. For the Haight would change over the next few months

San Francisco Examiner newspaper box ad, 1967.

from a discrete, psychedelic, neo-bohemian enclave into a crowded spectacle of some 10,000 resident hippies. Here's how Charles Perry, in his book *The Haight-Ashbury*, remembered Haight Street on a typical weekend afternoon in April 1967:

> Part Old Calcutta with beads and paisley-print fabrics and bare feet, incense and tinkling anklet bells, beggars squatting on the sidewalk. Part football stadium crush, complete with people selling programs—the *Oracle*, the *Barb* and two new papers, the *Haight-Ashbury Tribune* and the HA *Maverick*. Part Middle Ages, too, with a husband and wife evangelist team haranguing the crowds, and street dealers muttering their traditional street cry: "Acid, speed, lids?" There were conga drummers playing in front of the United California Bank and "sidewalk bikers," who aped the dress and mannerism of the Hell's Angels and the Gypsy Jokers, hanging out in front of Tracy's Donuts, waiting for the moment when their idols would roar up on their bikes through the traffic jam of tourists' automobiles. Once in a while the latest poem or screed or news flash or I Ching reading from the Communications Company would be handed out among the crowds up and down the street.

Naturally the big-city newspapers sent reporters, the national magazines sent writers, and CBS Television sent 44-year-old Harry Reasoner to produce a documentary called *The Hippie Temptation.* Reasoner tried to be even-handed. There was, he said, a sense of sharing, a peaceful attitude, some dedicated musicians. But he scolded the hippies for wanting adult freedoms without working, for imposing their ways on "straight" people in the neighborhood, for taking drugs but not always taking care of themselves—or each other. The hippies, he concluded, were children at play in the city.

Writers ten and fifteen years younger than Reasoner similarly struggled to comprehend what was surely the starkest display of the biggest generation gap in American history. Joan Didion (in *Slouching Towards Bethlehem*) saw Haight-Ashbury as "the desperate attempt of a handful of pathetically unequipped children to create a community in a vacuum." Didion exaggerated the problems, but

Barefoot hippies on Haight Street, 1967.

she accurately described the abuse of hallucinogenic drugs, the runaways who couldn't care for themselves and the rampant health and hygiene problems.

"Some hippies work," wrote Hunter S. Thompson in the *New York Times Magazine*, "others live on money from home and many are full-time beggars." The general lack of money, the spontaneous attractions on Haight Street, the daily pot smoking and weekly acid trips, the thousands of apartment floors that served as "crash pads"—all made formal entertainment (other than seeing the Dead at the Fillmore) almost obsolete. "The Haight-Ashbury scene," observed Thompson, "is almost devoid of anything 'to do'—at least by conventional standards."

Tom Wolfe enjoyed reporting from deep inside the acid experience, but he complained that even self-aware hippies had no philosophy other than warmed-over Buddhism mixed with Tolkien's *Lord of the Rings* and Huxley's *The Doors of Perception*. It was this lack of a goal or guiding principle—other than "just being"—that struck San Francisco writer Warren Hinckle as "the crisis of the hippie ethic." In *The Social History of the Hippies*, the left-wing Hinckle said "it is all right to turn on, but it is not enough to drop out." He couldn't abide thousands of middle-class hippies enjoying themselves in Haight-Ashbury while ignoring the Vietnam War and the civil rights movement.

Peter Coyote (née Cohon) was a founder of the Diggers, a group of well-educated and mostly well-off anarchists who tried to turn the Haight into a political movement. "I was interested in two things," he later told *Vanity Fair*: "overthrowing the government and fucking. They went seamlessly together." Coyote and his comrades did a lot more fornicating than overthrowing, but it probably did all seem to go together. The Diggers' big idea was "Freedom means everything free." They hated private property and believed money blocked "the free flow of energy." So they hassled Haight Street merchants, organized a Death of Money parade, and, for a few months, provided free meals in the Panhandle section of Golden Gate Park. With a pugnaciousness that sometimes caused altercations, they demanded end-cuts from butchers, leftover bread from restaurants, and wilted vegetables from produce wholesalers in order to make soups and stews for a couple of hundred people. Recipients of the free food walked through a wooden "Frame of Reference" to reorient their minds. The Diggers excelled in theatricality but failed in practical reasoning, and in the end converted few to their cause.

But it wasn't entirely their fault. The *San Francisco Oracle* was a popular psychedelic magazine that promoted "the freedom of the body, the pursuit of joy, and the expansion of consciousness"—that is, doing what you wanted, when you wanted, and with the help of pot and LSD. A widespread commitment to a philosophy of personal satisfaction hindered any effort at collective action.

Joan Didion got it right: the Haight-Ashbury was essentially a place of juvenile rebellion. One young man told her it was all about "doing a don't." And it was easy "doing a don't" in Haight-Ashbury: city authorities rarely hassled anyone; there was virtually no adult

Young woman selling the *San Francisco Oracle*, Haight-Ashbury, 1967.

authority; you could get by without a job; and most kids could always go back to college or send home for money. The whole scene infuriated a black preacher in a nearby neighborhood. "All we want for our people," he said, "is what these kids have given up."

Haight-Ashbury had already become a caricature of itself by the time 50,000 hippies, wannabe hippies, and curiosity seekers from across the country visited the neighborhood during the so-called Summer of Love. And when the summer visitors left, the scene collapsed. In October, a small group of original Haight-Ashbury hippies held a mock funeral ceremony they called "The Death of the Hippie." One of the organizers explained it this way: "We wanted to signal that this was the end of it, to stay where you are, bring the revolution to where you live and don't come here because it's over and done with."

If hippie culture proved unsustainable in the highly concentrated form of the Haight-Ashbury, it became perfectly viable when spread in small doses across the nation, where it answered a growing need for more personal freedoms and less formality. In an interview with *Rolling Stone* in 1970, Jerry Garcia said "The San Francisco energy of a few years back has become air and spread everywhere. It was the energy of becoming free, and so it became free . . . Today there is no place without its hippies. No place." That's even truer half a century later, when nearly everyone in America is a bit of a hippie.

7 City of Apps

The prototype of the lead player in today's San Francisco made his fictional debut more than thirty years ago in *The Golden Gate*, Vikram Seth's novel-in-verse about yuppies in the city. The novel's central character, John, lives in San Francisco but works in Silicon Valley, which

> Lures to ambition's ulcer alley
> Young graduates with siren screams
> Of power and wealth beyond their dreams,
> Ejects the lax, and drives the driven,
> Burning their candles at both ends.
> Thus files take precedence over friends,
> Labor is lauded, leisure riven.
> John kneels bareheaded and unshod
> Before the Chip, a jealous God.

Today it is San Francisco Apps rather than Silicon Valley Chips that lure the most ambitious young graduates—and inspire the city's latest impression of itself as a promised land. "For most of its brief life," wrote Richard Rodriguez in *Late Victorians*, "San Francisco has entertained an idea of itself as heaven on earth, whether as Gold Town or City Beautiful or the Haight-Ashbury." Rodriguez was writing about San Francisco in the 1970s and '80s, when its idea of itself as heaven on earth was as Gay Capital of the World. Today it would be the City of Apps.

The tens of thousands of driven young graduates who kneel before the App today, and who define so much of the city's tone, are but the latest surge of yuppies to hit San Francisco. The first surge hit in the 1980s. Back then, most yuppies came chiefly for the experience of living in the city after growing up in the suburbs and graduating from college. Others came for jobs in the expanding financial district. A few, like John, preferred to live in San Francisco while working in Silicon Valley. They all found cheap rent-controlled apartments in the Marina, Russian Hill, and Lower Nob Hill, or bought great old houses at low prices in Noe Valley, Cole Valley, and the Castro.

If nobody really noticed this first surge of yuppies—with their fern bars, croissant shops, coffee boutiques, video rental outlets, and computer stores—they came in much higher numbers during the 1990s and were a leading presence by the turn of the century. Some worked for dot-com firms in converted warehouses south of Market Street. Others worked in downtown banks, law offices, brokerage houses, engineering firms, and advertising companies. Still others worked for a growing city government and healthcare industry. Together they drove up prices for houses and apartments in a city that, by 2000, had regained the 100,000 people it had lost in the 1960s and '70s. While the majority of newcomers in the 1980s and '90s were Asian and Latino immigrants who settled in the Richmond, Sunset, and Mission, yuppies had higher education, better jobs, and more money—and thus made a bigger impact on the city.

This expanding group of (new, aging, and former) yuppies were part of a revivifying urbanity. They ate in new downtown restaurants like Boulevard and Kokkari, which still make northern California's version of European cuisine. They strolled along a waterfront that was opened up by tearing down the hulking Embarcadero freeway. They shopped at the Ferry Building, which was transformed into a high-end food emporium with a huge farmers' market. They helped fill every seat at every game in a new retro ballpark close to downtown. They rode vintage streetcars retrieved from storage in faraway cities and put back to work on Market Street. They took their dogs to Crissy Field, an old airstrip turned into a shoreline park. They visited the new Museum of Modern Art, the new Asian Art Museum,

The Hobart Building (built 1914) framed by late 20th-century towers.

HOBART
BUILDING

and SF Open Studios, the country's oldest (since 1975) and largest (800 artists by 2000) exhibition of artist studios. They gentrified Bernal Heights, North Beach, and Potrero Hill. They gentrified Hayes Valley once the Central Freeway was torn down. They gentrified some of the Mission, too, dining at Delfina's, buying bread and pastries at Tartine, eating tacos on 24th Street, and, in the process, begetting the Mission Yuppie Eradication Project, whose members specialized in making fliers calling for attacks on BMWs, sport utility vehicles, and hip cafés. And they went to the first Hardly Strictly Bluegrass, a spectacular three-day music festival that opened in Golden Gate Park in 2001 and is paid for in full, and in perpetuity, by a former San Francisco venture capitalist.

The pace of change accelerated over the next decade and a half, when another 100,000 people moved to the city and dozens of commercial and residential towers rose high above it. San Francisco is now ranked first or second (on a per capita basis) among American cities in college degrees, fitness centers, Airbnb listings, Uber riders, bicycle lanes, persons between the ages of eighteen and 34, fewest children, and fewest fast-food restaurants. San Francisco is also at the top in municipal spending, retail sales, money spent dining out,

Food carts and an eager line at the annual La Cocina Food Festival.

The street scene in Mid-Market now includes young techies.

median earnings among white workers, degree of tech savvy-ness (as measured by *Forbes*), and cost per square foot of commercial and residential real estate.

Most of the latest newcomers belong to a subspecies of yuppie called "techie." They numbered around 70,000 in 2017. Techies work a variety of jobs in the information and technology sector, which has accounted (directly and indirectly) for two-thirds of the city's employment growth since 2010 and pays an average annual wage of almost $120,000, nearly twice the city's average wage. Zendesk, Uber, Dolby, Square, and Twitter inhabit a stretch of mid-Market Street that, until a few years ago, was filled with drug dealers, donut shops, discount electronic stores, prostitutes, homeless people, and nonprofit organizations. Airbnb occupies a former jewelry mart a few blocks south. Yahoo took over the old *Chronicle* Building on 5th Street in 2013. Yelp leases a renovated Art Deco skyscraper not far from where Salesforce.com just moved into Salesforce Tower, the tallest structure west of the Mississippi. Dozens of smaller tech firms rent floors in buildings along the Market–Mission corridor between the waterfront and Civic Center. A new spa, taproom, cocktail bar, yoga studio, boutique bakery, specialty café, blow-dry bar, or wine, cheese and charcuterie place pops up every week to satisfy young tech (and tech-related) workers. Almost monthly, it

Anti-tech message spray-painted on sidewalk.

seems, you notice more stylishly scruffy young men in skinny jeans and untucked shirts, and more lithe young women wearing long hair and casual but expensive clothing.

It's impossible to ignore such a strong dose of the same kind of people in a compact city like San Francisco. An Asian American software engineer recently told the *New York Times* that he loves San Francisco but feels detached from the larger cycle of life: "It's similar to when you go to college and you are surrounded by people who are in the same life stage or who have the same attitude about what their priorities are. That's all you see: people who are exactly like you." Of course there are still plenty of working- and middle-class folks whose families have been here for generations. There are also plenty of former yuppies who came in the 1990s and are now middle-aged lawyers, doctors, teachers, architects, office managers, government employees, and small-business owners. Moreover, San Francisco is still one-third Asian and one-seventh Latino. Yet it's clearly the young graduates working for app companies who set the tone. Renderings of proposed residential and commercial buildings depict the new reality. The people in them are twentysomethings wearing small-brim fedoras and Henley shirts while riding bikes, looking at their phones, and ordering single-origin lattes from a coffee bar.

Most techies see San Francisco as heaven on earth: they earn good money, work high-status jobs in a leading industry, and enjoy the offerings of a sophisticated city in a beautiful setting. But not everyone likes the City of Apps. While the *Chronicle* and *San Francisco Business Times* generally treat techies with respect, writers in the *New Yorker*, the *London Review of Books*, and the *East Bay Express* have roughed them up. So did a documentary movie called *San Francisco 2.0*. *Salon* founder David Talbot overstates the basic complaint: San Francisco is in a conflict, he told *The Nation*, that "pits San Francisco's bedrock progressive values . . . against the defiantly individualistic, even solipsistic, world of digital capitalism."

Several facts help create the impression that techies are more capitalistic and individualistic than other San Franciscans. One is that techies are a conspicuous group of young, single, well-paid newcomers who work long hours but also spend a lot of time in upscale bars, cafés, and restaurants. What's more, techies are strictly business people, whereas many of San Francisco's former yuppies came in the 1980s and '90s as journalists, designers, architects, doctors, teachers, lawyers, therapists, government workers, or employees in nonprofit organizations. The image of techies has been sullied further by Uber's (and Airbnb's) mulish resistance to government regulation, and by several big tech firms that hired private buses to shuttle workers between San Francisco and Silicon Valley without seeking permission to use city bus stops.

But even if techies want more money and less government than other San Franciscans, they don't seem opposed to "San Francisco's bedrock progressive values." Most techies vote Democrat and support gay marriage, recreational marijuana, affirmative action, and carbon taxes. Nor are they likely to be more "individualistic" than other San Franciscans—if only because, as the British reformer Beatrice Webb noted long ago, individualism is an inveterate San Francisco trait. Many of today's middle-aged progressives, for instance, came to San Francisco as gentrifying yuppies and now send their kids to private schools. And many of the city's most progressive causes have expanded individual freedoms—to have sex, do drugs, dress as one pleases, remain forever in a rent-controlled apartment, live openly as a gay person, change your gender.

Most of the resentment against techies seems to be a matter of timing: they came to San Francisco just as several long-gathering difficulties became sizable problems. Techies began coming, for example, when housing prices were already the highest in the nation; when cars, buses, subways, and streetcars were slowing down; when almost every neighborhood was at least partly gentrified and nearly every pier, warehouse, and factory had been converted to new uses. And they came when new construction was already pushing many of the city's 8,000 homeless people out of once run-down parts of town and into more public places. Techies have surely accelerated the pace of change, and they've done so while hyping the benefits of their "disruptive" technologies. But techies didn't cause the problems: they've merely brought them to a head—a fact that didn't stop three supervisors from proposing a "tech tax" to fund more affordable housing and homeless services. One supervisor tried to justify the disingenuous proposal by saying "impacts should be borne by their impactors."

Nothing impacts San Francisco more than its high cost of housing. By 2016 two-thirds of its houses and condos were worth over $1 million, while the average monthly rent for a one-bedroom apartment was $3,500. It is estimated that only one in seven residents can afford the median price of a unit on the market. Because the high price of housing determines who can come and, in some cases, who can stay, it is fast determining whose city, and what kind of city, San Francisco will be. That's why housing is the most contentious issue in this very political city.

An ad during a recent election for district supervisor reflects the politics of housing. Backers of left-wing candidate Aaron Peskin mass-mailed a poster showing a smirking young white male in a sport jacket next to a big spread of $100 bills; the caption reads, "Who gets rich if Julie Christensen is elected?" The answer implied by the image is stated on the back: "Real Estate Speculators, Venture Capitalists and Developers." They'll get rich, the poster says, because Christensen is pro-landlord, anti-renter, and against regulation. (Although Christensen is not a left-winger, she would be considered very liberal almost anywhere else in the USA.) The deceptive ad played off the fear of losing one's apartment in a gentrifying city. It implied that techies are causing the housing crisis. And it got away with reverse bias: to have used a derisive stereotype of anyone other than a well-off (and straight-looking) white male would have immediately triggered accusations of racism, sexism, or classism.

The ad helped Peskin get elected because San Francisco is America's most liberal city, a fact verified by common sense for half a century and proved in 2014 by a statistical analysis in the *American Political Science Review*. Few San Franciscans, for example, consider an alternative sexual identity to be unconventional, never mind immoral. Immigrants are widely welcomed, and if they are here illegally the sheriff shields them from federal immigration authorities. A dozen groups specialize in protesting displacement, defending tenants, and promoting affordable housing. The city charges developers exorbitant fees because, a supervisor told me, "San Francisco is an attractive place to do business, so we make businesses pay a high cost for making money here."

Those fees help fund a municipal government that spends more money per capita than any other city government in the country. The annual budget for homeless people alone is more than $250 million, higher on a per capita basis than any other big city. Just as

Al and Tipper Gore looking at a section of the AIDS quilt in Washington, DC, 1997.

The Quilt

The *New York Times* wrote this about San Francisco's Castro district in July 1987:

> In this neighborhood that gained renown for its culture of openly expressed homosexuality, the predominant concern of the living is now dealing with death and dying. So many people have died of AIDS that many residents say they can no longer count the number of friends they have lost.

Later that summer several San Franciscans, led by Cleve Jones and calling themselves The NAMES Project Foundation, figured out how to count and commemorate their lost friends: with a quilt composed of individual "panels" made of lace, leather, cotton, and suede, and decorated with sewn images and small personal items. Each panel is 3 ft by 6 ft (0.9 m by 1.8 m)—the size of a human grave. The NAMES Project collected the individual panels and assembled them into sections which ultimately became the quilt.

In October that year the AIDS Memorial Quilt was displayed for a weekend on the National Mall in Washington, DC. Its 2,000 panels covered a space larger than a football field and were seen by almost half a million visitors. During a four-month, twenty-city tour in 1988, the quilt added enough panels to triple in size. Four years later it had panels from every state and 28 countries.

In January 1993, San Francisco recorded its 10,000th—*10,000th*—death from AIDS. The city honored its lost citizens with five minutes of silence and flags flown at half-mast. A week later The NAMES Project marched in President Clinton's inaugural parade.

The last display of the entire AIDS Memorial Quilt was on the National Mall in 1996. The quilt remains the largest ongoing community art project in the world. It's ongoing because AIDS continues to kill people. But it kills less often thanks to research conducted at San Francisco hospitals. And most of those with HIV today get sympathy because so many San Franciscans stood up for victims in the past.

San Francisco leads the nation in crafting progressive programs for homeless people, so too has it led the nation in creating policies like free needle exchanges for addicts and free "gender reassignment" surgery for uninsured people. The city is also a leader in banning things that irk specific supervisors—such as plastic bags, Styrofoam, McDonald's Happy Meals, and vending machines that sell candy bars on city property. The city even bans its agencies from doing business with companies that have yet to atone publicly for participating in the (pre-Civil War) slave trade. And it always elects a demographically diverse group of officials. In 2017 an Asian mayor worked with eleven supervisors: three Asian American females, two African American females, one Jewish female, one Asian American male, an Iranian American male and three white males, one of whom is gay and one of whom is Jewish.

But the city's progressives are facing a major problem: how to keep escalating housing costs from turning San Francisco into a city of upper-class people. One way is by staunchly defending the forty-year-old rent control law. Thanks to rent control, the high cost of housing affects mainly those who want to come to San Francisco, or, if they already live here, want to move to a better place. Rent control keeps annual increases below the rate of inflation unless a tenant voluntarily leaves, at which point the unit can be let to a new tenant at market rate. The unit is then subject to rent control at the market price until the renter leaves. Some landlords try to evict tenants illegally, but evictions are a small part of housing turnover because rent control is strict and the San Francisco Tenants Union is powerful. Because two-thirds of San Franciscans rent, and three-fourths of renters live in rent-controlled units, half the city's residents have an effective right of incumbency. But if rent control has slowed the shift to a wealthier class of renters, it cannot ultimately stop it.

So the city government is aggressively creating "affordable" housing for people earning up to 120 percent of the city's median income. It does so chiefly by forcing builders of condos and apartment houses to make about 25 percent of their units affordable—that is, subsidized. A builder can either include the affordable units in his otherwise market-rate building, construct an additional building made up entirely of affordable units, or pay a fee (or provide land) to the city, which then pays a nonprofit developer to construct the affordable units.

Affordable housing is great for those lucky enough to get it, but each affordable unit necessarily increases the cost of each market-rate unit. In essence, the municipal government is encouraging the building of high-end (and mostly high-rise) housing in order to get subsidized units for middle- and lower-income people. While progressives in the 1970s and '80s sought to curb growth and reduce building heights, progressives today promote greater height and density in order to get more subsidized housing and, they say, to increase the supply of housing so as to lower its average price.

But more building will not likely lower the cost of housing. For it's almost certain that San Francisco will continue to lure well-educated people, top-tier businesses and real estate investors. They will keep coming because San Francisco is the most attractive part of America's most dynamic region.

San Francisco may become too attractive for its own good, however. Since the late nineteenth century it has been a big city with a light touch, a busy but free-flowing metropolis, a mix of urban vitality and easy living. For well over a century, in other words, the city has been marked by a feeling of relaxed intensity.

The feeling has a physical cause: countless views, a perfect density, and mostly low, soft-colored buildings. Since 1990, however, San Francisco has added 150,000 people, nearly as many jobs, and a lot of cars to its streets, passengers to its transit system, and highrises to its skyline. It has added several million more tourists as well; on any given day, one in twelve people is a visitor. And it has developed, or is in the process of developing, every empty lot, open space, and abandoned warehouse. Naturally the city feels more crowded, cramped, and congested.

The city's relaxed intensity has a social cause, too. While San Francisco has always had a lot of high-powered business people, it has also had strong countervailing actors like labor unions, community activists, urban conservationists, and all sorts of bohemians. But the fast-paced culture of money-making is starting to overwhelm all resistance to it. And the city's politicians are nearly as frenetic as the capitalists. The push by left-wing politicians for more jobs, housing, and office towers—and the new tax revenues they generate—has become an end in itself. All the while every new development is fought bitterly by those who might get displaced, or don't want their neighborhood to change, or hope to enlist a politician to extract a bigger pay-off from the developer. San Francisco's relaxed intensity has suddenly become more intense than relaxed.

And if the city's beauty still staggers even casual observers, parts of San Francisco are losing their looks. To come into the city over the Bay Bridge, or by ferry from Oakland, is to confront a wall of glass that is mainly green, mostly undistinguished, and relentlessly growing. The big shiny mass envelops old skyscrapers and hides the hills beyond it. And it's not just downtown that is getting higher, greener, and shinier. Clumps of tall buildings are spreading up Mission and Market Streets, around Civic Center and along Van Ness Avenue. Entire sections of the city's rolling topography are being obscured and visually flattened by glassy high-rises.

Glass skins on steel frames are marvels of engineering. As pure forms, they can seem impressive—especially from a distance. But they are faceless. They lack the details and textures that give older buildings a recognizable expression that is always individual, often enticing, sometimes beautiful. What's more, the metallic greens and glossy silvers of today's high-rises flout the century-old advice of Arthur Page Brown, architect of the Ferry Building. San Francisco's pale light, he suggested, calls for a corresponding lightness of color in its buildings: soft pinks, shades of white, a range of flat beiges and greys. If Brown were alive today, he would surely insist that any building tall enough to block views of the Bay Bridge, of Telegraph Hill, of an Art Deco skyscraper, of a part of the bay, or a piece of the sky, had better be awfully good to look at.

Make no mistake about it: San Francisco is still "The Cool, Grey City of Love" in George Sterling's poem; the "dazzling, exotic, and curiously romantic" city in H. L. Mencken's *San Francisco: A Memory*;

Downtown's growing wall of glass as seen from Mission Dolores Park, 2017.

San Francisco as seen from the Berkeley hills at dusk.

the enchanting Baghdad-by-the-Bay in Herb Caen's newspaper columns. And in the last decade or so, the city has added public treasures like the de Young Museum in Golden Gate Park, the Contemporary Jewish Museum on Mission Street, the Exploratorium along the Embarcadero, and a new wing to downtown's Museum of Modern Art, which holds the prodigious Fisher collection of contemporary art. But if San Francisco keeps luring more high-end businesses and greater numbers of highly educated people, it will keep getting richer, taller, glassier, denser, and tenser. The benefits of such growth will come at the cost of qualities that have long made San Francisco so distinctive and pleasing: its hilly beauty, its quirkiness, its relaxed intensity, its openness to different kinds of people, and its many points of view, both physical and social. Such qualities are rarely obtained, easy to lose, and hard to live without—at least for those who have been lucky enough to know them.

THE CITY TODAY

Shrine for a young man killed in a gang fight.

24th Street

Few neighborhoods comfortably blend social classes, ethnic groups, and natives and immigrants. And when they do, it's rarely for long. An exception is San Francisco's Mission District, which is framed by Potrero Avenue and Mission Street on the east and west, and 16th and Cesar Chavez on the north and south. For sixty years now the Mission has successfully combined whites with Latinos, foreigners with Americans, and blue-collar workers with white-collar employees.

Mexicans started moving to the Mission around 1950, when it was home to second- and third-generation Irish, Germans, and Italians who shopped along Mission and 24th Streets and worked on the waterfront and in neighborhood factories. The *San Francisco Chronicle* wrote a series of articles about the Mission in 1962. Despite some run-down Victorians and a handful of residents who disliked the new immigrants, the general picture was one of a quietly changing neighborhood in which hard-working Latinos were embraced by the churches and welcomed with *Se Habla Español* signs in white-owned stores. By the end of the decade, Mexicans, Salvadorans, and Nicaraguans made up a third of Mission residents. They worked mainly on landscaping crews, as house cleaners and dishwashers, and as janitors and housekeeping staff in downtown hotels and office buildings. A couple dozen Latinos even joined with white neighbors to form the Mission Coalition Organization, which successfully fought city plans to redevelop the neighborhood.

The Mission acquired a distinctly Latino flavor in the 1970s. The teacher of a Latino studies class at San Francisco State (the very first university to open an ethnic studies program) helped students create a bilingual newspaper for the neighborhood. Local organizers founded community groups to provide legal and medical services to new immigrants. Latino entrepreneurs took over stores and restaurants on 24th Street and Mission Street. Artists began painting the murals that now decorate a stretch of 24th and several adjoining alleys. Some murals are serious and political, others light and festive; all celebrate Latino culture with images ranging from low-riders and Carlos Santana to Mayan peasants and Frida Kahlo.

The Mission hit its peak as a *barrio* in the early 1990s, when Hispanics made up the majority of residents, owned most of the stores, and ran the churches. Grandparents, children, and grandchildren often lived on the same block, sometimes in the same building. Second-generation Salvadorans and Mexicans cruised the streets in low-riders. Elaborate wedding parties spilled from churches onto sidewalks. *Quinceañera* celebrations regularly took over restaurants. Gangs fought over street corners. Immigrants still arrived in large numbers. Whites and Latinos had the same median incomes.

The Mission today would be nearly all Latino if not for the influx of yuppies that began in the mid-1990s and accelerated after 2010. The Mission now has more whites than Latinos. The median price of a house rose from $280,000 in 1990 to nearly $1 million in 2015. Mission whites now make 50 percent more than Mission Latinos.

Although thousands of Latinos bought houses in the 1960s, '70s, and '80s, and rent control shields most apartment dwellers from rent hikes and evictions, young adults who grew up in the Mission can rarely afford to leave their parents' place and stay in the neighborhood. Moreover, white newcomers who buy three-story Victorians from Latinos can lawfully evict any renters with the standard San Francisco pay-off—anywhere between $5,000 and $50,000—before fixing up the house and moving in. All the while, rising rents have curbed the arrival of new immigrants.

The storefronts on 24th Street reflect the changing composition of the neighborhood—the street between Mission and Potrero is ten straight blocks of small businesses serving the district's main Latino section. Ten years ago, Latinos owned more than four of every five businesses; today they own about two of every three. They own nail and hair salons, produce and meat markets, real estate firms and tax attorney offices, travel agencies and money-wiring operations, several *panaderias* (pastry shops), and most of the restaurants. They also run nonprofit operations that provide daycare, medical services, pre-school education, and gallery space for local artists. Whites own the three book stores, several swanky bars, cafés and restaurants, and a juice bar, a boutique clothing store, and a work-out spa.

By all accounts 24th Street is safer and busier than it was fifteen years ago, but the accelerating shift to a whiter and wealthier set of stores, shoppers, and residents has created an underlying tension that surfaced a few years ago at Local's Corner, a white-owned and upscale restaurant that opened in 2012. A waiter told a party of Latinos what he told other parties when the place was full: they could wait for a table or go to a sister restaurant a few blocks away. But the would-be customers took offense. One said to the waiter, "Hey, we're locals, too, man," playing off the name of the restaurant. Another quickly sent emails saying they had been turned away because they were Latinos. The real trouble began when the bilingual neighborhood paper, *El Tecolote*, ran a story favoring the accusers. After that, members of an outside empowerment group got involved. They put up posters showing the restaurant owner's face next to the word "boycott." A small group of demonstrators picketed the restaurant and called the owner a racist. The owner refused to sign a list of demands about whom he should hire and how he should treat his workers and customers. Somebody threw bricks through his storefront window and tagged it with graffiti: "Die Yuppies," "Get Lost" and "Keep the Mission Brown." This was the work of a small number of people—some of them from outside the Mission—who exploited unease about changes in the neighborhood. The owner closed his restaurant.

Like other parts of San Francisco, the Mission has been gentrifying; but the incident at Local's Corner was an extreme reaction to it. So I asked about fifty people on 24th Street what they thought about the changes in their neighborhood. Their responses fell along three main lines.

A white yuppie and a second-generation Latina.

A half dozen people—all of them young, educated, second-generation Latinos—took the line that the Mission belongs to Latinos. Among them was the editor of *El Tecolote*. This American-born son of Mexican immigrants questioned the tactics of those who criticized Local's Corner, but he agreed with them that "outsiders should respect the local culture." The restaurant's owner, he told me, should have made a special seating arrangement for the Latinos who wanted to eat at his restaurant on that fateful day. "Why?" I asked. Because they had been living on 24th Street for a long time, he said, and deserve respect. What's more, he said, outsiders should hire Latinos, be sensitive to their ways, and contribute to the culture of the neighborhood, which, he emphasized, is a *Latino* culture.

That's also the official position of Calle 24, a group of local artists, merchants, and political activists whose self-proclaimed purpose is to preserve the neighborhood as a Latino neighborhood. They recently got the Board of Supervisors to designate 24th Street a Latino Cultural District. Their stated goal is to "ensure that new development in San Francisco's Mission District responds to and reflects the traditions and cultures in the Latino Cultural District." To that end they want to restrict new market-rate housing, build subsidized housing for Latinos, and use city funds to retain and attract "culturally relevant businesses," a euphemism for Latino-owned.

Nearly half of those I spoke with on 24th Street have mixed feelings about the changes in their neighborhood. Take the example of a brother and sister who own the *panaderia* their Mexican parents opened in the early 1970s. The middle-aged siblings don't want neighbors evicted from apartments by yuppies who buy Victorians, but they acknowledge that the sellers are Latinos. Nor do they like watching the neighborhood lose its Latino identity, though they recognize that it's not all bad. "I'll be sad if Spanish and the *panaderias* and the *carnicerias* go away," the brother told me. "So I give back to the neighborhood by hosting Spanish-language poetry readings in our shop. And I provide pastries and coffee." But he admits that the mostly young white newcomers have made 24th Street cleaner and more prosperous. And his sister is proud of her

Neon sign for Panaderia Mexicana bakery.

college-educated daughter who married a *gringo* and left the *barrio*. The siblings are planning to close their shop and rent out the space. They will have to decide whether to rent to a Latino business for less money, or to a white entrepreneur who will pay a lot more to set up a bar, restaurant, or exercise studio.

A slight majority of the shoppers, strollers, and shopkeepers I spoke with took the line that cities are in constant flux, and that the decline of Latino culture on 24th Street is nothing to lament. Most of the white (and Asian American) newcomers naturally took this line, but so did many Latinos. So too did a thirty-year-old Middle Easterner who has lived most of his life in San Francisco and now runs a shabby corner store that sells soda, cigarettes, liquor, lottery tickets, and basic household items. He's been working at the store, which his father set up, since he was a boy. He likes the well-off newcomers. Though they rarely shop at his store, they've made the neighborhood safer: the gangs are gone, he told me, and so are the prostitutes and drug dealers. He clearly doesn't mind that the Mission is becoming less Latino, and he doesn't think Latinos should mind either. "I'm an immigrant like them," he told me.

And like them, my family came here to find something new and better. And we all stayed because it *is* better. I guess it's all right to hold onto your old culture for a while, but eventually you have to let it go—at least some of it. It's kind of weird to keep holding on to the old world that you or your parents left behind to come here. Besides, no single group can own a neighborhood forever. This neighborhood wasn't always Latino, you know. So you have to go with the changes. You can't stop it anyway.

The Tenderloin

"It may be too strong to say I love the Tenderloin," wrote Herb Caen in the 1970s, "but I dig it. Every city should have one. Going a step further, any city that doesn't have a Tenderloin isn't a city at all." The Tenderloin is still full of what Caen saw in the 1970s: "rundown blocks, rundown people, rundown apartment houses." But I "dig it" now like Caen dug it then.

The Tenderloin lies in the heart of the city, between Union Square and Civic Center. It is full of handsome but run-down apartment buildings occupied mainly by poor people renting studios and one-bedrooms. The poorest people rent tiny rooms—most of which lack private bathrooms or kitchens—in single-room occupancy hotels (SROs). The streets are lined with coffee and donut shops, old-style lunch counters, Vietnamese restaurants, dive bars, pawn shops, and massage parlors. There are plenty of liquor stores, corner stores, and second-hand stores, but hardly any produce stores.

Blacks, whites, Asians, and Latinos live in the Tenderloin in about the same proportions as they live throughout the city. But in the Tenderloin there are three males for every two females, the average person earns one-sixth of the city's median income, six out of seven adults aren't living in families, and half of its people are unemployed and receive public assistance. At almost any point in the day you'll see people waiting in lines for some kind of service. Thousands eat breakfast and lunch at St Anthony's and Glide Memorial Church. A few hundred homeless people take afternoon naps in the pews of St Boniface church. Dozens clean themselves in city buses that have been converted to mobile showers. Others get

Street scene at the Page Hotel.

free care or counseling at Tenderloin Health Services, Hospitality House, and the Tenderloin Housing Clinic.

Outsiders don't always feel comfortable. To walk two or three blocks in the Tenderloin is to pass several homeless people, a few prostitutes, a couple of drug dealers, and someone injecting himself. But you'll also see Vietnamese kids being walked to school by parents or grandparents who came as refugees in the 1970s and '80s. Most of all, you'll see people passing time. Small groups stand on corners, take over stoops, and set up milk crates and folding chairs on sidewalks. An outsider rarely feels danger or hostility, but he typically feels uneasy about the disorganized and sometimes desperate lives all around him.

So why do I dig today's Tenderloin like Herb Caen dug it forty years ago? As a San Franciscan, I believe the city should have room for all kinds of people. As a walker, I take a (perhaps voyeuristic) pleasure in seeing the underside of urban life while learning something about people normally out of view. As a person open to unexpected encounters, I find the Tenderloin the most likely place to have them. Most encounters are trivial, others are off-putting, some are friendly but fleeting. Every so often, however, I actually get to know somebody quite different from myself.

Two years ago, for example, I was taking pictures in the Tenderloin when a guy leaning against a nearby mailbox said, "You better leave, man. Nobody wants you taking pictures around here. That group over there," he said, pointing his head in the direction of five or six people across the street, "they're dealers and pimps. They'll fuck you up for taking their pictures."

He was a burly black man about my age. He wore a black windbreaker, sunglasses, and two rhinestone earrings. I walked over to him and said I was taking pictures for classes I teach. "I don't give a goddam who you are or why you're taking pictures," he said. "I'm

Volunteers giving manicures to Tenderloin residents.

telling you for your own good. If they see you they'll take your camera and fuck with you. I'm just telling you. Do what you want." I pretended not to be rattled. "I live further up Jones Street and walk through here all the time," I said, "but thanks for the warning." I asked if he lived nearby. "Look man, don't be asking me no questions." Then I asked about the particular corner we were standing on. "I told you, man; I ain't answering no questions." Just then a middle-aged white guy walked by. He was scruffy and high. The black guy yelled at him for not paying back the $20 he'd lent him, and scolded him for wasting money on drugs. The white guy shrugged and shuffled away, saying over his shoulder that he'd pay him back next week.

The black guy suddenly started complaining about all the drinking and drug use in the Tenderloin. He told me that he used to be an addict, and homeless too, but had been "clean and sheltered" for five years now. He even helped out a few days a week at an Alcoholics Anonymous office down the street. He lived in an SRO two blocks away. We talked for a few more minutes, shook hands, and exchanged first names. I told him I'd come by some time for a cup of coffee. "Okay," he said. "I usually hang out a block away, at the corner of Ellis and Jones. You can find me there."

A few weeks later I found Ronnie on the corner. He looked surprised. He'd forgotten my name but accepted an invitation to lunch. Since then I've seen him every two or three months. I can almost always find him at the corner, where, he says,

> it's like watching television. You know, it's all a bunch of soap operas and crime stories out here. I'm sober and don't sell drugs or hustle people no more, so I just watch it all happening. When I first got off drugs I didn't think anything would ever be interesting again. But it is. Even more so sometimes.

When he's not at the corner I look for him in the tiny Alcoholics Anonymous office where he volunteers. If he's not there, he's usually sitting in the sad lobby of his SRO hotel.

Over lunch he talks about growing up in the Fillmore, living on the street, his stint in jail, and the "three love children I made on drugs," one of whom he's in touch with. He's proud of himself for quitting alcohol and drugs, yet he wonders if he'll ever get off welfare. His only other source of income is selling pirated DVDs. I tell him about teaching, my father's dementia, and living for a few years in Latin America. And we talk about women. Sometimes we talk about Black Lives Matter. Ronnie doesn't read much, but he watches a lot of news on television and he watches his busy street corner. He's a smart guy and an easy talker who knows something about life.

When the check comes he always laughs and says, "Now you know I don't mind you paying because you're a professor, a $100,000 man. I'm just a welfare man." But he offers to buy the 99¢ coffees we pick up at a tiny shop run by a Mexican immigrant. Ronnie and I intersect only at the fringes of our lives. But we enjoy the intersection. And it happens in the Tenderloin.

Ronnie wouldn't be living there today if political activists hadn't pushed the city to preserve the Tenderloin as a neighborhood for poor people. In 1979 the city made it illegal to destroy SROs or convert them into tourist hotels or apartment buildings. Since then, a combination of social services and housing organizations have

Residential hotels Jefferson, Fairfax, and Kinney.

Elderly women lining up for free food.

stabilized the Tenderloin as a kind of high-functioning slum. A fifth of the buildings in the Tenderloin are owned by nonprofit organizations that use city funding to offer below-market rents. Other buildings are owned by private landlords who rent mainly to tenants on government assistance. Still other buildings are privately owned but leased to nonprofits whose tenants pay rents with city funds and welfare checks.

Over the last five years, however, big money and well-off people have been squeezing the Tenderloin. Technology companies, refurbished hotels, residential high-rises, and upscale restaurants now set the tone along Market Street between 5th and 11th, the old southern border of the Tenderloin. In the last couple of years the northern border has shifted from Geary Boulevard to O'Farrell Street. And there are fewer truly isolated and dangerous blocks than there were just two or three years ago. The borders will retreat further as young people earning good money replace poor tenants in the best

Tenderloin apartment buildings, and as art galleries and boutique bakeries replace liquor stores and auto-body shops.

Yet it's unlikely that the Tenderloin will ever be fully gentrified. Much of its housing stock is reserved for poor people, and most college graduates don't want to share sidewalks with SRO tenants like Ronnie or live next to welfare recipients in rent-controlled buildings. The neighborhood will definitely tip further, however, and a new balance will have to be found. Peter Field worked for years with intellectually disabled people in the Tenderloin. Today he gives walking tours of the neighborhood. "As a social worker," he told journalist Gary Kamiya, "I want to do everything in my power to protect people from the landlords who would throw them out. They're evil motherfuckers. But as a San Franciscan, as a guy who likes to walk, I want all this stuff cleaned up." But not so cleaned up that it's no longer the Tenderloin. Like Herb Caen said, a city without a Tenderloin isn't a city at all.

Bike messengers taking a break at Market and Montgomery Streets.

Ride Tough or Go Home

"**A**nd to think there are those who do not admire our mad bike messengers," wrote Herb Caen in 1983. "They never cease to amaze, amuse, and frighten me." San Francisco is a great city for messengers: the hills make it exciting; the weather makes it pleasant; the wealth makes it viable. And there are plenty of individuals mad enough to ride.

A 1985 *People* magazine article about San Francisco bike messengers describes the madness:

> Call them what you like—concrete cowboys, scourge of the streets or the unsung heroes of corporate communication—San Francisco's bicycle messengers are a hair-raising breed apart. Like trigger-itchy desperadoes, these steel-steeded carriers, some 400 strong, slice through traffic, running red lights, nicking pedestrians, swerving to avoid open car doors and lane-changing drivers. They pump furiously up lung-searing inclines, then streak down from hilltops, just to make yet another routine delivery to the quiet confines of office America.

The description is hyperbolic, but it fits my memories of working as a messenger for half a year in 1979. There was a certain fury to the riding—cars paid no attention to bikes, messengers broke all the rules, cops hassled us—and the average messenger positively enjoyed his reputation as a hellion of the streets.

A dozen of us met every Friday after work at the Hotel Utah bar to trade stories from the week—about seeing another messenger slam into a door flung open from a parked car; about sliding underneath a big truck after wiping out on wet trolley tracks; about hitching a ride up California Street by holding onto the rear corner post of a cable car. One messenger saw a fellow rider crushed against a parked car by a tractor-trailer making a tight right-hand turn. A couple of true daredevils bragged about breaking side-view mirrors with their handlebars while speeding between rows of cars stopped at a light.

And there were stories about a motorcycle cop named McClellan, who liked to chase us down and ticket us for riding on sidewalks, ignoring stop signs, and going the wrong way on one-way streets. I got ticketed twice in six months. We rode fast and broke rules—the maxim was Ride Tough or Go Home—because we got paid half the price of each "tag," or delivery. But if McClellan saw plenty of infractions, he didn't always get the culprits. Our best stories were about escaping him—by turning into a narrow alley, riding through a plaza, or heading down a one-way street.

A common feeling we rarely talked about was voiced by a messenger in the *People* magazine article. "Some people," he said,

> think we're the scum of society. I once walked into a Bank of America and these four people were standing there completely ignoring me, talking about this problem they were having in marketing. Now, I got my degree in marketing. I wrote a paper on the problem they were discussing. They hadn't mentioned one important theory that would have applied to their problem, so I stepped in and brought it up. There was this deadly silence. I handed them the package, and they signed for it right away. I really enjoyed that.

Whenever I thought a businessman in an elevator was looking down at me as a bike messenger, I made sure he saw whatever book I had with me that day, a book he probably hadn't read, like *The Autobiography of Malcolm X* or *Slaughterhouse-five* or *The Crying of Lot 49*. That even secretaries and receptionists saw us as slightly feral only increased the camaraderie we felt about doing a job most others wouldn't do.

A messenger today still rides a "tank bike" built for Aero Delivery in the 1970s.

Bike messengering was at its peak between the late 1970s and the late '90s. Although fax machines and email began cutting into deliveries in the early '90s, strong growth in an expanding financial district made up for losses. During the first decade of the new century, however, faster Internet connections and web-based services like DropBox and DocuSign drastically reduced the need for paper copies of everything from checks, contracts, and plane tickets to blueprints, financial reports, and legal filings. Various messenger companies went out of business, and at least 200 riders went with them. In 2008 *Wired* magazine published an article called "Internet Endangers Big-city Tradition: The Bike Messenger." No city had proportionately more messengers—or a bigger Internet economy— than San Francisco.

But messengering is coming back. Over the last several years a number of new companies and another hundred messengers have

SAN FRANCISCO

returned to the business—though it's a rather different business. Most new companies use start-up partnerships and logistical apps, and most messengers deliver consumer items to individuals instead of documents between businesses. Prepared food is the main item, but messengers also deliver flowers, a bottle of wine, a pair of shoes, an iMac from the Apple store, accessories from a sex shop, even the occasional latte. Every month, it seems, some start-up invents an app for delivering another item by bike. An industry once dependent on the needs of businesses now relies on the desires of consumers.

The work of messengers has changed with the shifting market for deliveries, as I learned by talking to riders who take breaks on the steps at Market and Montgomery Streets. Today's shoulder-bagged messengers ride their own bikes instead of the company bikes—single-gear Schwinns with big baskets or short "tank" bikes with fold-up trailers—that were ridden by earlier generations. And if previous messengers abused company bikes by hopping curbs and dropping them on the ground when getting off for deliveries, today's riders respect their bikes and know how to maintain them. Many even have second bikes for recreational riding and racing. In fact, today's messengers need to be better cyclists because they go on long runs all over the city instead of many short hops around the central business district.

A lanky, taciturn, grey-bearded 55-year-old named Raymond, who started riding in the mid-1980s, told me that today's messengers "are still weirder than the average person—more tattoos, more pot smoking, more distrust of authority, more voting libertarian or Green—but they aren't as weird or intense as riders were twenty or thirty years ago. Riders will always have a streak of recklessness in them," he continued, "because nobody aims for this job; they just fall into it for two or three years—except for a few like me, who fall in but never get out. But today's riders are definitely more sensible and less rebellious." I asked if he knew the maxim Ride Tough or Go Home. "Sure," he said, "back in the day. But it's not like that anymore. Don't get me wrong: most civilians still look down on messengers, and riding is still hard and sometimes dangerous. But it's not as wild as it used to be."

When I asked why, he said more of today's riders have been to college and they now deal with customers who tip instead of employees who sign for packages. "But the biggest difference between riding now and riding twenty or thirty years ago," he said, "is that it's much easier and safer to ride today, which probably attracts a saner group of messengers. There's a lot less antagonism between bike riders and car drivers, and the cops hardly bother messengers anymore. And that's mostly because of Critical Mass."

Raymond was referring to the large groups of cyclists who rode through downtown during the evening commute on the last Friday of every month. The event began in 1992 and was originally called the Commute Clot, but it was as much a chaotic celebration of biking as it was a protest against the difficulties of riding in the city. Sixty bikers rode in the first event, a thousand rode a year later, and 2,000 or 3,000 typically rode in the late 1990s. By 2003 some 300 cities around the world had versions of San Francisco's mass rides.

The originators of the event wrote a pamphlet in 1994 called "How to Make a CRITICAL MASS: Lessons and Ideas from the San Francisco Experience." It shows how to set a route, block traffic, keep the group together, and deal with police. And it explains its origins: "The idea was initially conceived by one person, who bounced the idea off other cyclists. San Francisco's prominent bicycle messenger community was enlisted primarily through word of mouth, while [bicycle] commuters were reached by someone standing in the middle of the financial district passing out flyers."

A long-time bike messenger named Junior gave a bawdier account of its origins:

> It all started when a bunch of drunk bike messengers got tired of San Francisco police handing out $20 tickets to cyclists all the time for bullshit minor offenses, like not putting your foot down at a stop sign. $20 was a big chunk of your take-home pay way back then, so they decided to shut down some key intersections around the city and show the cops they couldn't just fuck with them. Seems to have gotten their attention.

Counting cyclists in a bike lane on Market Street.

Junior's account is part truth and part myth-making, but Critical Mass definitely got the city's attention. After Mayor Willie Brown called Critical Mass "an incredible display of arrogance" in the summer of 1997, a particularly raucous Critical Mass of some 5,000 riders caused enough chaos to convince the city to create its first bicycle transit plan and expand its bike lanes.

Critical Mass crusaders made the moderate San Francisco Bicycle Coalition a big player in city politics. Critical Mass is now an occasional minor spectacle. The Bicycle Coalition has over 10,000 members and helps plan the city's bike lanes, which now total 125 miles (200 km). According to *Bicycling* magazine, San Francisco is the country's second-most-friendly city for cyclists.

"People who ride bikes today take for granted all the bike lines and bike racks," says Raymond, "as well as their right to share the streets with cars that generally yield to them. They don't know all the work that older cyclists and bike messengers did to make it that way. Every techie riding to Twitter on a nice bike lane has some lowly old bike messenger like me to thank for it."

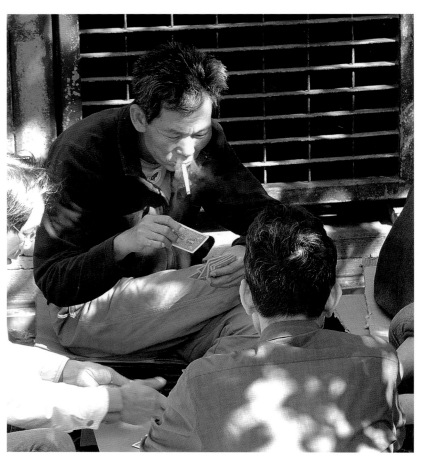

Playing cards in Portsmouth Square.

Chinatown

There is nothing remarkable about being Chinese in San Francisco today. A quarter of the city's residents claim Chinese descent, and they live all over the city. The kids and grandkids of Chinese immigrants make up the majority of students at Lowell High School, one of the nation's best. Chinese Americans hold top posts in the city government.

Yet Chinatown is still, as Herb Caen said half a century ago, "the city's most fascinating and authentic foreign colony"—exactly what Mark Twain and Bret Harte said a century before Caen. The segregated Chinatown of tong wars, opium dens, and pigtails is long gone, but Chinatown today seems more like a Chinese village than an American neighborhood. It is 95 percent Chinese, 75 percent of whom are foreign-born. And it is poor: one-third of its residents live below the poverty line. Nearly everyone who works in Chinatown is Chinese, and nearly every piece of private property is owned by someone of Chinese descent. Most job postings and rental listings are in Chinese characters only. Even Chinese Americans from other parts of San Francisco view Chinatown as an exotic and foreign land.

But if every visitor to Chinatown finds it "fascinating," few see anything "authentic." That's because most visitors go to see one event, the Chinese New Year's Parade, or to see one street, Grant Avenue. San Francisco's Chinese New Year's parade is the largest and oldest outside of Asia. The three-hour procession has big corporate sponsors and looks like a cross between a Chinese lantern festival and an American parade. Miss Chinatown USA, umbrella twirlers, martial arts performers, dozens of colorful floats, hundreds of big animal costumes, and a 300-ft (90-m) dragon conveyed by a hundred hidden puppeteers all move through the streets amid a relentless din of cymbals, drums, and firecrackers. Grant Avenue is less dramatic but similarly staged. For it is lined with pagodas, lanterns, restaurants, souvenir shops and jewelry stores, and the only Chinese people on it are shopkeepers selling to tourists. Grant Avenue cuts through the heart of Chinatown, but it is cut off from the neighborhood.

You can easily see the real Chinatown, however, just by leaving Grant Avenue and walking along Stockton, Pacific, Clay, and Washington. You'll see a nearly unbroken chain of cheap stores and restaurants on the first floors of run-down buildings whose tenants occupy tiny apartments, share bathrooms and kitchens, and hang laundry from windows and fire escapes. You can walk down any one of a dozen alleys to glimpse a basement barbershop, a small sewing factory, or a little meeting hall with twenty people sitting on folding chairs. And you can go to Portsmouth Square to watch women do t'ai chi while their chain-smoking men play cards on pieces of cardboard. Almost everyone is speaking Cantonese.

Because most residents occupy tiny rooms in multistory buildings, Chinatown is five times denser than San Francisco as a whole.

Public notice at a fish store.

A typically crowded Chinatown street corner.

It feels even denser. Thousands of small stores, most with their own signs or awnings, create an impression of terrific commercial density. Because half of Chinatown's people are over 55, and most older folks don't work, they seek relief from stuffy apartments by spending large parts of their days hanging around Portsmouth Square and cheap restaurants. Most eateries are small and simple, have English-translation names like Five Happiness, and are filled with Chinese customers eating noodles, dumplings, steamed buns, and various rice dishes. And because many apartments are too small for pantries and refrigerators, a lot of women shop every day in cramped stores that sell all manner of unusual fruits, fish, vegetables, and dried foods. Produce bins extend onto narrow sidewalks already jammed with shoppers and pedestrians hoping to avoid workers pushing handcarts between stores and double-parked trucks. The apparent lack of tacit rules for easing movement—rules like forming lines at checkout counters or keeping to the right on sidewalks—makes Chinatown feel all the more crowded.

Laundry day.

Chinatown would be less Chinese today if not for a small group of Chinese Americans who became political activists in the 1970s and '80s. They kept the city from tearing down the local hospital that served poor, Chinese-speaking residents. They stopped the demolition of old apartment buildings and single-room occupancy hotels. They pushed the planning department to place height limits on new buildings. They defended tenants against unscrupulous landlords. They forced the city to provide Chinatown with Chinese American cops and firefighters, and with adequate bus service, street cleaning, and senior housing. And they registered people to vote, got Chinese Americans appointed to city commissions and departments, and eventually got one of their own into the mayor's office.

The nature of Chinatown's property market has also helped keep Chinatown a good place for poor immigrants. Old-time family associations own about 40 percent of Chinatown's buildings, and it's hard to get multiple families to agree to sell jointly owned property.

Ethnic Chinese individuals own another 40 percent of Chinatown's buildings, and because hardly any of these long-held properties have mortgages, or pay high property taxes, their owners have less incentive to raise rents—or improve their properties. Most of the neighborhood's other buildings are owned or operated by nonprofit groups that serve poor people.

A Chinatown alley.

But not even Chinatown is immune from San Francisco's rising rents and property values. The long-time Chinese owners of a single-room occupancy hotel, for example, recently sold their building to an outside real estate company. The company fixed up the bathrooms and corrected code violations before serving eviction notices for, among other things, hanging laundry on fire escapes. Activists marched in front of the building waving signs that said "Doing laundry is not a crime." Community leaders procured the help of Mayor Ed Lee, a former advocate for immigrants and affordable housing, to force the new owners to rescind the eviction notices.

Political pressure can stop evictions, and rent control slows turnover, but nothing can prevent property owners from raising rents for new tenants. Nor can anything prevent long-time owners of commercial buildings from selling to outsiders. When a six-story building overlooking Portsmouth Square recently went up for sale, the head of the Chinese Chamber of Commerce reacted to the news: "If tech offices invade Chinatown buildings, there is no way our community-serving merchants can compete with them on rent. We will be driven out of Chinatown." The founder of the nonprofit Chinatown Community Development Corporation agreed: "We cannot afford to have this building turn into a technology center. It will raise rents for everybody" and encourage an influx of "hipsters."

Consider as well the upscale Chinese food emporium that just opened on Broadway. The three-story complex includes the Oolong Café, the Gold Mountain Lounge, the 888 Banquet Room, and the Marketplace store, which sells teas, spices, and cookware. But the main attraction is the Market Restaurant, which claims to offer "a daily changing seasonal menu cooked from eight specialized stations that merge traditional Chinese and Western culinary equipment. A main dining area plays centerpiece, appointed with chairs and tables all handcrafted in China from reclaimed Chinese elm." A Chinatown business advocate told the *Chronicle* that,

> for the locals, it's going to be overpriced, but it does give people from other neighborhoods an opportunity to come back to Chinatown like in the 1940s and 1950s. There's high hopes from

some of our more professional people who want to revitalize Chinatown at night.

San Francisco's Chinatown is America's longest-lasting ethnic enclave. It endured decades of official prejudice. It rebuilt itself after a devastating earthquake. It hit its peak of prosperity and socio-economic diversity in the 1940s and '50s before losing many of its best restaurants and better-off residents in the 1960s and '70s. Since then it has been a good place for poor Chinese immigrants. But rising property values pose a real threat to Chinatown's survival as a cultural enclave.

Twenty years from now thousands of poor Chinese will still inhabit tiny rooms while millions of tourists continue to walk along Grant Avenue. But increasing numbers of college graduates will also be renting upgraded apartments, working for start-ups in converted buildings, and ordering lattes at fancy cafés—while professionals from all over the Bay Area visit Chinatown to eat Westernized Chinese food in retro-themed restaurants. For the first time, it's actually possible to imagine Chinatown as something other than what Herb Caen called it half a century ago: "the city's most fascinating and authentic foreign colony."

Statue of Gandhi at the farmers' market.

Gandhi at the Farmers' Market

"With the possible exception of New Orleans," writes the *Washington Post* food critic, "no American city obsesses more about food—buying it, cooking it, eating it, talking about it—than San Francisco." He's almost certainly right.

Northern California's Mediterranean climate and multiple ecosystems have always supplied San Francisco with a wider array of fresh food than any other American city. And the city's cooks have always created foods that other Americans like: think of sourdough bread; crab Louie; Ghirardelli chocolate; Rice-a-Roni; the seafood stew cioppino; the fried egg, bacon, and oyster mix called Hangtown fry; and Anchor Steam beer, the nation's first modern craft brewery. Starting in the 1970s, San Francisco chefs joined Berkeley's Alice Waters to create "California cuisine" and initiate a widespread movement for fresh, seasonal, organic, and locally grown ingredients. San Francisco today has proportionately more restaurants and fewer fast-food places than any other city in the country. It offers fine dining in elegant downtown restaurants, as well as authentic ethnic food—like Vietnamese pho, Salvadoran papusas and Chinese dim sum—in the Tenderloin, the Mission, and the Richmond. Newfangled taprooms, cocktail bars, and boutique bakeries are everywhere.

So are farmers' markets. There are two dozen in San Francisco alone, and half are open all year round. One in particular epitomizes the high-end food culture that has become mainstream eating for many San Franciscans, and nicely shows the city's obsession with food.

The farmers' market that surrounds the beautifully restored Ferry Building on Saturday mornings typically draws 20,000 people

Young farmers at their produce stand.

who walk through a high-priced cornucopia of perfect food: fresh fruits, herbs, and vegetables; local nuts, honeys, and berries; specialty breads, artisanal cheeses, just-butchered meats. Vendors hang signs certifying their organic accreditation, and they display info cards about the farms that grow the food: their owners, their location, their sustainable methods. You can even leave your groceries with the "veggie valet" while eating a porchetta sandwich near a music student playing a Bach cello suite.

Such gustatory delights seem at odds, however, with the image of Gandhi—who stands on a pedestal in the middle of the market wearing a robe and carrying a walking stick. A kid who saw me taking a picture of the Mahatma asked his mother about him. "He was a man who believed in peace," she said, "not in fighting wars." She nicely evaded the incongruity of the ascetic Gandhi in the sumptuous market.

Yet it's not impossible to reconcile Gandhi with the market: just as he was an enlightened and spiritual man, so is the market an enlightened and spiritual place. That, anyway, is the attitude of the market's organizer, the Center for Urban Education about Sustainable Agriculture. CUESA believes deeply in the old adage "you are what you eat." In fact, CUESA has expanded its meaning to include not only *what* you eat, but who grows it, where it's from, and how it's made—all of which affects your relationship to the planet, to your community, and, most of all, to yourself.

CUESA works hard to enlighten you about food and eating at its Ferry Building market. It offers lectures about nutrition and farming in the age of global warming. It uses interactive exhibits to help you picture sustainable food systems. It gives classes on knife-handling and butchering. It organizes cooking demonstrations by San Francisco chefs. It makes vendors exhibit laminated info cards about their farms. And it hands out pamphlets at its information booths— pamphlets about what's in season, which chefs buy at the market,

Selling organic, vegan, gluten-free tofu products.

and how to understand the confusing array of animal welfare labels. There is even a pamphlet called "10 Tips for Waste Wise Shopping." Tips range from "Bring your own bags" and "Buy only what you can reasonably eat" to harder ones like "Bring your own plate, cutlery, cloth napkin, and beverage container" so as to "avoid single-use items."

It's clear that a lot of people go to the market for more than groceries: they go as a kind of spiritual and political practice. Going to the market shows your commitment to the small, to the local, to the organic, the artisanal, and the sustainable. The market empowers you, says CUESA, to "protect the environment through your purchasing." And it helps you to build a community around "the town square, where chefs, farmers, food makers, and food lovers come together to talk produce and grow a healthy food system together."

While some people go to the market just to see beautiful food, buy a bag of fresh peaches, and eat a piece of rotisserie chicken while looking at the Bay Bridge, most are fully into the spirit of the thing. No other city, after all, has a higher share of progressives or foodies—or progressive foodies. For them food is a personal statement as well as a culinary experience. Just as they like talking to vendors about a rare strain of tomato, the provenance of a cheese, and the humane raising of animals, so do they like buying organic food from small local farms using sustainable methods. And they are happy to pay a lot of money for it. What Gandhi would say is anyone's guess.

Connecting the Homeless

Project Homeless Connect was set up in 2004 as part of a new, gentler, more expensive way of dealing with the city's 8,000 homeless people, about half of whom sleep on the streets, half in shelters. By any measure, that's a lot of homeless people. It seems even higher because many of them hang around public spots like Civic Center, Hallidie Plaza, and the eastern edge of Golden Gate Park.

By providing services to people on the street, Project Homeless Connect improves their lives while easing the burden on emergency rooms, where a lot of homeless people seek medical attention, and on the fire department as well, which handles most emergency medical calls. Project Homeless Connect's most spectacular offering is an all-day event for about 1,500 street people. The event takes place every few months at the Bill Graham Auditorium in Civic Center plaza.

About an hour before homeless people start coming through the doors, several hundred volunteers sign in, put on Project Homeless Connect T-shirts, and get seated for a "rally" in a section of the auditorium balcony. We can see workers on the big floor below us setting up two-dozen service stations for everything from eye exams and photo IDs to blood tests and drug counseling. The Singers of the Street open the rally. This small choir of formerly homeless people sing "Help!" and "Bridge over Troubled Water" and "On the Sunny Side of the Street." The mayor follows the singers with a speech trumpeting the city's efforts to help the homeless. The event coordinator then reviews our job instructions and counsels us to refrain from using "he" or "her" out of respect for those who don't think of themselves as male or female. Specific groups of volunteers cheer when the coordinator thanks the business, organization, or college that is sponsoring them. About two-thirds of all volunteers come with a group; the rest come on their own. Most volunteers are either middle-aged or in their twenties, and are mainly white with a strong contingent of Asian Americans. Although God is never mentioned, and seems to inspire but a few, the air is thick with righteous enthusiasm for helping those less fortunate than oneself.

I go downstairs with forty other volunteers to a large room off the main floor. Our job is to check-in homeless people, find out what they need, and hand them off to volunteers who escort them

City bus converted to a mobile shower.

to service stations on the floor. Once the doors open I talk to one homeless person after another, about forty in total, for several hours.

Each person sits across from me at a long narrow table. I tell them I need some information before sending them in for services. I take down their names, note their birth dates and social security numbers, and record their cellphone numbers. I find out if they've served in the military or spent time in an orphanage. I ask them how long they've been homeless and where they go for medical care. Then I ask them their sexual orientation. I don't like asking this question because some of them don't like answering it. It's even harder asking whether they identify themselves as male, female, or transgender. Many of them don't understand the question. Some are miffed. One woman cupped her breasts and said, "I'm a woman, fool! Can't you tell?" But everyone answers because everyone wants something.

When I ask what they need, the desperate ones lift their shirts to show an infected rash or a colostomy bag, or they open their mouths to reveal an abscess. Most simply say they need to see a doctor or a dentist, or would like a haircut and a pair of reading glasses, or want a foot wash, an identity card, and clean needles. Everyone wants the free lunch and bag of groceries, and many are looking for clothing. After making a list of their needs, I ask to look at the four-digit number on the wristband they received when entering the building. Like a child showing his mother a cut, each person obediently extends his arm so I can read the number. I then call a volunteer to escort the person to specific service stations on the main floor. Some thank me as they leave, most just move along.

The first four or five people I interview always make me alert— to their smells, to their anxiety, to their drug addiction, to their psychological problems, to the obvious wear and tear, physically and mentally, that living on the streets exacts upon them. At the last event I worked, the first person who sat across from me was a gay Latino in his early twenties. He was tense, dirty, hard-edged. He spoke fast and avoided eye contact. He could barely stay in his chair. He wanted an HIV test. The second person was a sixty-year-old white man wearing several layers of clothes on a warm day. He was a polite alcoholic who had been on the streets for fifteen years. He wanted a haircut and reading glasses. Next came a thirty-year-old black woman. She was highly agitated and probably high. She said she was a prostitute and wanted condoms and needed to talk to somebody about her "mental problems." A ten-year-old girl then sat down. Her mother stood behind her. The girl spoke limited English but had almost no accent. The mother didn't speak English at all. So we spoke Spanish. They had been in San Francisco for a week after making an overland journey from Honduras. The mother stiffened when a policeman walked by. I assured her that he wouldn't arrest them. The girl needed new glasses. I convinced the mother to see somebody about getting her daughter into school, and to use the free phone service to call home. As soon as they left, a well-spoken man of thirty took the seat. He was clean-shaven, had clean fingernails, and wore clean clothes. But he was gaunt and looked distant and weary. He'd been sleeping in a shelter for a couple of months. "I want needles," he said, "and to talk to a drug counselor."

By this time, about thirty minutes into it, I was barely smelling their smells or registering their distress. I wasn't even seeing them as homeless people; they were just people who needed help. It's partly a matter of getting used to it, but it's mainly about checking one's impulse to make judgments.

San Francisco's Project Homeless Connect has been copied by cities across the country. It's run by caring people and supported by thousands of volunteers. And it's just one part of a vast operation to help the city's street people, an operation now under the direction of a new Department of Homelessness, the first in the nation.

In the last fifteen years the city has placed a few thousand street people in long-term housing, mainly in single-room occupancy hotels. It has operated shelters for several thousand others. And it has paid for bus rides home for 2,000 or 3,000 more, though nobody knows how many of them have come back to San Francisco. At the same time, the city provides all manner of medical, mental, and counseling services. Street outreach teams search for those most in distress. Mobile shower buses let street people clean up while mobile veterinary clinics treat their animals. Even the police treat

GIVE ME YOUR TIRED, YOUR POOR, YOUR HUDDLED
MASSES YEARNING TO BREATHE FREE, THE WRETCHED
REFUSE OF YOUR TEEMING SHORE. SEND THESE,
THE HOMELESS
TEMPEST-TOST TO ME
I LIFT MY LAMP BESIDE

Mural on a homeless shelter.

homeless people with care. All of this costs money: San Francisco's budget for homeless services in 2017 was over $250 million—more than that of the Public Works Department, twice that of the public library system, and equal to $30,000 per homeless person.

Yet the number of homeless people today is the same as it was when Project Homeless Connect started in 2004. There is a core group of several thousand chronically homeless people with drug, alcohol, or mental health problems who prefer living and sleeping on the streets. There are several thousand others who live on the streets by day and sleep in shelters at night, but who would move to permanent housing if it were made freely available. Nobody knows exactly how many street people became homeless while in San Francisco, and how many came to the city with no means of support. So I conducted a survey of 200 homeless people. Seventy percent came to San Francisco already homeless or on the verge of homelessness. And they came to San Francisco because it's a good place to be homeless—which helps explain why every homeless person helped off the streets is replaced by another.

Sign taped to a building.

As I left the auditorium and cut across Civic Center plaza, I saw volunteers from Project Homeless Connect watching the dogs and cats of homeless people who were still inside. Someone was hawking *Street Sheet*, the country's longest-running and largest-circulating street paper. Dozens of homeless people were lounging on the steps of the library. Dozens more, I knew, were inside, where they've virtually taken over the main bathroom. By the time I had walked three blocks up Larkin Street, and had sidestepped a fresh pile of human feces and passed another fifteen homeless people, a few of them huddling together to smoke meth, I was losing the sense of connection I'd felt in the auditorium.

Fifteen hundred street people, 700 volunteers, a dozen permanent staffers, two or three policemen—all of us in the auditorium that day were on our best behavior. Feelings of hope and kindness overcame feelings of revulsion, shame, and disapproval. Inside the Auditorium, street people weren't a problem: they were individuals with problems. Back on the streets, however, it was hard to see them as individuals, to refrain from making judgments, to consider them as something other than a collective nuisance. But I had to try.

Urban Retro

San Francisco was the first American city to recover from the urban downturn and ugly architectural modernism of the 1960s and '70s, and it did so by returning to the past—a mainly brand-new past. During the 1980s and '90s, San Francisco installed old-looking street lamps downtown and returned vintage streetcars to Market Street, with a sign on each car telling where it last served: 1940s Boston, 1950s Philadelphia, 1960s Cincinnati. Skyscrapers in the 1980s and '90s applied neoclassical decoration, borrowed Art Deco forms, or combined pieces of those styles. Empty lots in the factory district south of Market Street were filled with "live-work units" that evoked industrial times with their glass bricks, exposed I-beams and sheet-metal facades. Young professionals moving into converted warehouses liked seeing the faded names of former wholesalers still painted on the sides of their buildings; if there weren't any old advertisements, developers painted them on so they looked old. Gentrifiers of century-old neighborhoods (in Bernal Heights, Potrero Hill, Noe Valley, and the Mission) restored brick and stone, hung carriage lamps, and installed new kitchens and bathrooms while retaining original molding, light fixtures, and doorknobs.

The area around New Montgomery and Howard Streets offers what a condo developer there calls "the art of urban living." By this he means the urbanity we associate with American cities of the 1940s and '50s: a neon martini glass hanging outside a chic club, a remodeled lounge in a boutique hotel that advertises itself as "a genuinely retro bar," and a "supper club" that, according to a San

Retro barbershop.

Francisco magazine, promises to "transport us to a time past when food, drink, and music was all enjoyed under one roof in a dimly lit, lounge-like atmosphere." The developer was also selling the idea of a short stroll to the new retro ballpark, where Tony Bennett serenades fans after every win with "I Left My Heart in San Francisco."

Although the latest residential and commercial high-rises prefer sheer glass to historical decoration, every new "taproom," "speakeasy" and "barber and shop" displays old photos of the building, old maps of the city, and old drawings of the craft of brewing or distilling or barbering. Similarly, new print shops use traditional equipment to make stationery, insignia, and business cards for firms that, a printer told me, "value authentic machines and work practices." The Workshop Cafe on Montgomery Street is filled with young businesspeople paying for high-speed Internet and shared space with other digital entrepreneurs. The café describes itself as an "evolving platform for creation that can power your start-up and work dreams." Yet its logo is an old-fashioned gear. Dozens of new restaurants have old wooden booths, art nouveau chandeliers, restored neon signs, Art Deco-like lamps, and the inevitable film noir posters in their bathrooms. The bathroom door in one such place has a mail slot. Originally it might have been a door to an apartment building—or maybe it was just made to look as if it was.

Twitter occupies a beautifully renovated furniture mart on Market Street. A display of old mailboxes adorns the lobby. The accompanying plaque says, "The bronze mail boxes are original to the 1937 Art Deco building and were relocated from the old mail room . . . This use of 'found art' reminds us that finding new purposes for older buildings and their materials is an inherently sustainable practice." That's an excellent sentiment—though the plaque fails to remind us

Vintage Philadelphia streetcar turning onto Market Street.

Old mailboxes at Twitter.

that technologies like Twitter helped finish off the letters that once filled the mailboxes.

The retro zeitgeist is on full display at Sightglass, a fetching coffee house in an old warehouse south of Market Street. Its exposed rafters, wrought-iron railings, and rustic-cut table tops suggest the work of craftsmen in small shops. Many employees wear knit caps and lumbermen's shirts. Others chain their wallets to their belts. Some have the job of pouring raw beans from burlap bags into a vintage 1958 cast-iron coffee roaster that sits like a museum piece in the middle of the café. (The café's name, by the way, comes from the term for the roaster's viewing window.) Old-style lettering on an office door recalls the era of Dashiell Hammett and Sam Spade. A classic hi-fi system plays vinyl albums. One-pound bags of coffee for sale display the name and location of the "artisanal" grower: "We believe," says Sightglass, "that knowing the story behind your coffee—where it was grown, how it was processed, and who handled it along the way—is a powerful link from the cup to the wider world." The patrons of Sightglass are mainly young laptoppers working in nearby tech start-ups. It's hard to know if they feel a powerful link between their cup of coffee and the "traditional" Colombian farm that grew the beans. They almost certainly miss the irony of disruptive app-makers surrounding themselves with old-fashioned things.

It's all a rather audacious bit of nostalgic overkill, but whether it's real or not is irrelevant to those who buy the lifestyle—though it does create interesting contradictions. Take, for example, the gentri-fied neighborhoods that have been transformed so quickly, and by such similar kinds of people, that they are often as homogeneous, with respect to age, race, income, and education, as a 1950s suburb. Some gentrifiers acknowledge this lack of diversity, and it's a pain-ful admission because "diversity," after all, is what they say they like about the city. One such person told the *Chronicle* that he wished Noe Valley had kept some of its "working-class charm." The phrase is telling, as if the picturesque working man were just another feature of the real estate, like water towers or exposed brickwork, that might be preserved for the benefit of gentrifiers and their property values.

There's probably no single cause of the retro style that San Fran-cisco has been pioneering for three or four decades now. But it seems clear that American cities hit their peaks as aesthetic objects—as collections of buildings, streetcars, storefronts, and skylines, and as centers of urbanity, too—in the late 1940s and '50s. So it makes sense to restore or recreate old things that look good rather than invent new things that look bad. That's surely why San Francisco planners and architects in the 1980s and '90s rejected the modernism of the 1960s and '70s and worked to preserve old structures, replace freeways with boulevards, and design buildings with historical decoration. That American cities once looked better also helps explain why so many interior decorators and product makers blend elements of old styles. A designer of small apartment buildings told me that "design today is all about collage, like sampling in hip-hop." And what better way for yuppies to be urbane than by spending money to demonstrate their sense of history and connoisseurship—if only for straight-razor shaves in retro barbershops, specialty cocktails in old-style speakeasies, and single-origin coffee roasted in vintage roasters? Whatever the cause of urban retro, it now seems as natural as the city's fog.

Street *Litter*ature in Lower Nob Hill

There is a type of litter that is also a kind of literature: handwritten notes thrown away on city streets by their writers or readers. I've found hundreds of them in San Francisco over the last 25 years. I find them on sidewalks mostly, but sometimes in alleys, or against street curbs. The notes fall into three main categories: from largest to smallest, the categories are grocery lists, to-do lists, and neighbor-to-neighbor messages. Electronic devices are curbing the need for handwritten notes, but people still write them—and they keep landing on the streets.

I find them mainly in Lower Nob Hill, a thirty-block section of handsome five-story apartment buildings between upper-class Nob Hill and the lower-class Tenderloin. Dashiell Hammett lived in Lower Nob Hill during the 1920s, and set his *Maltese Falcon* there. It's always been dense, full of small stores, home mainly to single people and childless couples, and, for those reasons, the best neighborhood for finding discarded notes.

Like most San Francisco neighborhoods, Lower Nob Hill has become wealthier and younger in the last ten years. Landlords renovate their apartment buildings. Taprooms, work-out spas, and cute restaurants replace local bars, lunch counters, and convenience stores. One-bedroom apartments now rent for $4,000. Yet the replacement of lesser-off residents by better-off residents has been gradual and remains incomplete. Rent control protects the older folks, the small-time professionals, and the nurses, plumbers, and artists who moved to Lower Nob Hill before rents shot up in the late 1990s.

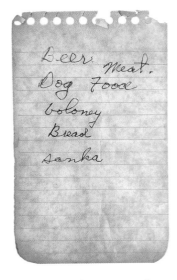

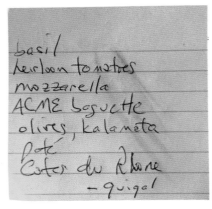

So a wide variety of people still write notes that end up on the streets of this "trending" neighborhood, as the realtors call it. The author of the grocery list on white lined paper, for example, is probably an older person who has been renting the same apartment for thirty years and doesn't use the list-making app on his iPhone—if he has one.

Most grocery lists are fancier, and tend to consist of ingredients for a meal. The list on a yellow post-it for an appetizer or light supper made me realize, when I found it a few years ago, that the neighborhood was indeed "trending." Corner stores that in 2010 didn't carry high-quality baguettes, never mind good but moderately priced French wines, are now carrying mozzarella and heirloom tomatoes as well.

The first to-do list opposite (on two post-its) is dated and includes tasks for the day as well as for the week. Who is this woman who does yoga and smokes a blunt before knitting, and is about to get her insides cleansed and her tongue pierced? She could be a twenty-year-old barista working at a hip coffee shop while going to art school and sharing a one-bedroom apartment with two roommates, each paying $1,300 per month. But she knits. So maybe she's a New Ager going through a mid-life crisis in a rent-controlled apartment she got in 1990. And what happens, by the way, at the end of the month? That's the beauty of the found note: the writer is unknown, so the finder invents the story.

The author of the second to-do list could be working in the tech sector and sharing a two-bedroom apartment for $5,000. If so, she probably walks to work near Civic Center or takes one of the private "Chariot" buses to a tech zone in SOMA, the South-of-Market district. Young tech workers in sales and marketing departments make $80,000 per year, which after taxes comes to $5,000 per month, at least half of which goes on rent. So she buys her clothes at Nordstroms but saves money on household items at Target. The items on many to-do lists are numbered, and they are usually checked or crossed out as tasks are finished; and like this one, they are often amended over time: "shower" and "arms & abs" were written later in pencil.

Some to-do lists propose larger goals instead of discrete tasks or errands. I've found a dozen lists urging their writers to become better organized or get a promotion or form a start-up. The author of IMPROVEMENT SHEET could be a yuppie internalizing the workplace optimism of a tech company's sales department, or a middle-aged

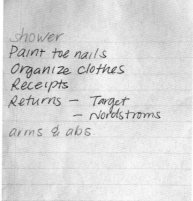

interior designer talking to a life coach. Americans are the masters of self-help programs, goal planning, and improvement projects. And San Franciscans are surely among the best at self-motivating: most have come from elsewhere, after all, with the goal of succeeding in a highly competitive environment.

While "high quality local electrician" is not strictly a to-do list, it is probably the first step in making a work résumé. The electrician has probably been working (and perhaps living) in the neighborhood for twenty years, but he's now competing for jobs offered by young entrepreneurs who are opening fancy restaurants and remodeling apartment buildings that have their own web pages. To get work today he needs a résumé, a presence on Yelp, maybe even a website. The electrician is an example of the difficulties that middle-aged, working-class people face today in San Francisco. A barber who opened his shop on Bush Street in 1975 had to close it in 2010. He couldn't afford the higher rent, he told me, and "young guys today don't want an old barber anyway. But they sure like those retro barbershops. Hell, I can give a better straight razor shave than any of them."

The last to-do list—more like a note-to-self, actually—was written by somebody who makes money by pulling cans and bottles

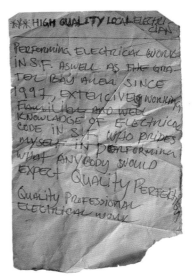

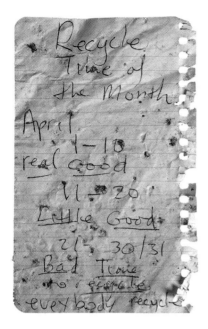

from sidewalk trash bins in Lower Nob Hill. She probably lives in Chinatown. I say this because I often see older Asian women hauling garbage bags full of cans and bottles. The author of *Recycle Time of the Month* writes that it's "<u>real good</u>" to collect during the first third of the month, "<u>Little Good</u>" the middle third, and "<u>Bad Time</u>" the last third. That's because people on supplemental social security and general assistance get their checks on the first of the month, and they tend not to gather recyclables until they get low on money. This particular recycler knows her market for cans and bottles.

Unlike grocery lists or to-do lists, neighbor-to-neighbor messages are meant for someone else. Many of them concern parking, which, as the note below implies, is a big problem in San Francisco. Parking messages land on the street because, as I've seen several times, the recipient removes it from the windshield wiper, reads it, and drops it. Most other neighbor-to-neighbor messages display a similar corrective tone. Just as you can feel Jerome's annoyance with the cigarette butts, so can you picture Steve tossing away the message that he probably found stuck to his mailbox in the foyer.

What could be more trivial, really, than a shopping list, a to-do list, or a note from one neighbor to another? But each note necessarily reveals something about its author—as well as the culture of San Francisco. Its anonymity gives it a heightened, abstract quality, which, in turn, lets it exemplify a *type* of person, behavior, or attitude. And its very detachment from its source gives it the advantage of a novel over a movie, or a black-and-white photo over a color photo: the advantage of letting the viewer make the most of his imagination.

LISTINGS

Hotels

Mark Hopkins Hotel

999 California Street

www.intercontinentalmarkhopkins.com

The nineteenth-floor penthouse suite was converted in 1939 to the glass-walled Top of the Mark restaurant and lounge, which offers sweeping views of the city and its surroundings. The Room of the Dons features nine large mural panels about California's history painted by Maynard Dixon and Frank Van Sloun.

Palace Hotel

2 New Montgomery Place

Enjoy high tea in the high-domed Garden Room, and drink a cocktail in the Pied Piper Bar and Grill, which features a big Maxfield Parrish painting of the Pied Piper of Hamelin luring a group of kids.

Fairmont Hotel

950 Mason Street

www.fairmont.com

Beyond the stately lobby is the Tonga Room and Hurricane Bar, which in 1945 became one of the country's first tiki palaces.

Clift Hotel

495 Geary Street

www.morganshotelgroup.com/originals/originals-clift-san-francisco

The Redwood Room was paneled with wood from a single redwood tree, which also supplied the lumber for the exquisite bar. The Redwood Room still has Art Deco lamps and etched brass doors, but the huge reproductions of Gustav Klimt paintings have been replaced by digital art on giant TV screens.

Huntington Hotel

1075 California Street

www.thescarlethotels.com/huntington-hotel-san-francisco/

The plush hotel bar is frequented by Nob Hill regulars, many of them older than the average San Franciscan, and it is filled with the sounds of classic American songs played by a pianist.

The bar leads to the Big 4 Restaurant, an old-style room adorned with historical photographs.

Vintage Bars

Vesuvio

255 Columbus Avenue

www.vesuvio.com

The bar was established in 1948 as a bohemian meeting place. Kerouac, Ginsberg, and Ferlinghetti drank there. Francis Ford Coppola composed the *Godfather* screenplay there. Most of its employees are working artists.

The Saloon

1232 Grant Avenue

www.sfblues.weebly.com/saloon-schedule.html

Established in 1861, The Saloon is probably the oldest bar in SF. It features live music, mostly blues, and once hosted Janis Joplin, Jefferson Airplane, BB King, Johnny Otis, and Aretha Franklin.

Mr. Bing's Cocktail Lounge

201 Columbus Avenue

Chinatown's best dive bar is small and cluttered but full of interesting people with stories to tell.

Elixir

3200 Sixteenth Street

www.elixirsf.com

Built in 1858, this handsome local saloon has been beautifully restored with a mahogany bar, leaded windows, and wood paneling.

Aub Zam Zam

1633 Haight Street

The place has been serving cocktails for eighty years. It was opened by an Assyrian immigrant and has twin minarets, Moorish archways, and a colorful king-and-princess mural behind the circular bar.

Twin Peaks Tavern

401 Castro Street

www.twinpeakstavern.com

The bar is at the center of the Castro neighborhood near the turnaround for old-time streetcars running up and down Market Street. New owners in 1972 installed full-length plate-glass windows, making it the first gay bar in America whose patrons were fully visible from the street.

The Hotel Utah Saloon

500 Fourth Street

www.hotelutah.com

The Utah was built in 1908 as a bar and lodging house. It attracted beatniks and gamblers in the 1950s, gay men in the '60s, and bike messengers in the '70s. It has live music most nights, and hosts the longest-running open-mic night in California.

House of Shields

39 New Montgomery Street

www.thehouseofshields.com

Across the street from the Palace Hotel, the House of Shields is a handsome bar with nicely refurbished booths, glass sconces, mosaic-tiled floors, and spectacular woodwork. It attracts downtown's young business crowd.

Museums

SF Museum of Modern Art
151 Third Street
www.sfmoma.org
The SF MOMA opened in 1996 as the first west-coast museum dedicated to contemporary art. The MOMA recently completed a major expansion for displaying works from the prodigious Fisher Collection of contemporary art.

Palace of the Legion of Honor
100 34th Avenue
https://legionofhonor.famsf.org
The Palace was built in 1924 as a full-scale replica of the French Pavilion from the 1915 Pan-Pacific International Exposition. It has a broad collection of mainly European art, and is located on a bluff above the Pacific with views of the Golden Gate Bridge.

De Young Museum
Golden Gate Park
https://deyoung.famsf.org
The de Young showcases North American art as well as artworks from Africa, the Pacific, and the rest of the Americas. The museum's new building in Golden Gate Park is clad in copper, which will eventually turn greenish and blend with nearby eucalyptus trees. A twisting observation tower gives panoramic views.

Walt Disney Family Museum
104 Montgomery Street, Presidio
www.waltdisney.org
A wonderful new museum in the Presidio about the life and work of Walt Disney.

49 Geary Street Art Galleries
This is the single best place to visit galleries in San Francisco. Four floors exhibit the works of first-rate painters, sculptors, and photographers.

Gallery Japonesque

824 Montgomery Street, Jackson Square
www.japonesquegallery.com
A two-level gallery dedicated to the exquisite arrangement of a wide
variety of contemporary Japanese art.

Pier 24 Photography

Embarcadero, Pier 24
www.pier24.org
The permanent collection of the Pilara Foundation is housed at Pier 24.
The Pilara Foundation puts on one or two big exhibitions per year in the
spacious setting of a renovated pier shed.

Contemporary Jewish Museum

736 Mission Street
www.thecjm.org
The Jewish museum occupies a former substation and works with other
institutions to present artistic and scholarly exhibitions about the Jewish
experience.

Cable Car Museum

1201 Mason Street
www.cablecarmuseum.org
The museum is housed in the operating cable-car powerhouse, and has a
collection of old cable cars, machinery, equipment, and photographs.

California Historical Society

678 Mission Street
www.californiahistoricalsociety.org
The Society was founded in 1871 and has been open continuously since
1922. It holds diaries, journals, letters, photographs, business records,
oral histories, paintings, catalogs, and all manner of Californiana.

The Beat Museum

540 Broadway

www.kerouac.com

A quirky collection of more than 1,000 photographs, posters, books, paintings, and other artifacts from the Beat experience.

California Academy of Sciences

55 Music Concourse Drive, Golden Gate Park

www.calacademy.org

With some 25 million specimens, it is among the world's largest museums of natural history.

Tenderloin Museum

398 Eddy Street

www.tenderloinmuseum.org

A museum that displays photographs, videos, and artifacts about the history of a dense, sometimes troubled, and always fascinating neighborhood.

Music Venues

The War Memorial Opera House

301 Van Ness Avenue

www.sfwmpac.org

Opened in 1932 as one of the last Beaux-Arts structures built in the United States, it is home to the San Francisco Ballet and the San Francisco Opera.

Davies Symphony Hall

201 Van Ness Avenue

www.sfsymphony.org

The hall opened in 1980 to house the San Francisco Symphony Orchestra.

Nob Hill Masonic Auditorium

1111 California Street

www.sfmasonic.com

This white, modernist, streamlined building has a huge mosaic window displaying Masonic ideas and images; the auditorium hosts musicians and public speakers.

SF Jazz Center

201 Franklin Street

https://sfjazz.org

The Center opened in 2013 and was billed as the west coast's first freestanding structure built strictly for jazz.

The Fillmore Auditorium

1805 Geary Boulevard

www.thefillmore.com

The Fillmore has been a dance hall, a skating rink, and, most famously, the favored venue for the Grateful Dead.

The Warfield

982 Market Street

www.thewarfieldtheatre.com

Opened in 1922 as a vaudeville and movie palace, it has an ornate lobby loaded with marble, chandeliers, and a grand staircase, and has featured everyone from Al Jolson and Louis Armstrong to Dylan, the Dead, the Clash, and U2.

The Great American Music Hall

859 O'Farrell Street

www.gam.com

Rolling Stone magazine called the Great American one of the nation's best small concert halls for rock 'n' roll. It was built in 1906 as an ornate restaurant and bordello, and still has its old-fashioned marquee, ceiling frescoes, and oak floor.

Freight & Salvage Coffeehouse
2020 Addison Street, Berkeley
www.thefreight.org
This folk-music emporium was opened in 1968 in a used furniture store.
The Freight is now a nonprofit community arts organization, and one
of the very best places to see various forms of traditional music from all
over the world.

Restaurants

Chez Panisse
1517 Shattuck Avenue, Berkeley
www.chezpanisse.com
Alice Waters's Berkeley restaurant opened in 1971 and inspired the style
of cooking known as California cuisine, which uses fresh, seasonal, local,
organic ingredients.

Zuni Café
1658 Market Street
www.zunicafe.com
Set up in 1979, Zuni was one of the first restaurants to display raw brick
walls and exposed beams, and to make modern use of a wood oven to
cook pizza and roast chicken. Zuni brought the Chez Panisse style to San
Francisco.

Tadich Grill
240 California Street, Buich Building
www.tadichgrill.com
This old-style downtown seafood restaurant opened in 1849 as the New
World Coffee Saloon before becoming the Tadich Grill in 1887. It's been
owned by the Buich family since 1928.

Mario's Bohemian Cigar Store Café

566 Columbus Avenue

Enjoy excellent sandwiches, coffee, and beer in a great spot on Washington Square in North Beach.

Limón Rotisserie

1001 South Van Ness Street

www.limonrotisserie.com

This Peruvian restaurant in the Mission features moist rotisserie chicken with delicious sauces, and dozens of small eclectic plates.

Z & Y Restaurant

655 Jackson Street

www.zandyrestaurant.com

This is where to get spicy Sichuan food in Chinatown. Two items from the menu are Chicken with Explosive Chili Pepper and Salty Pepper with Prawns.

Presidio Social Club

563 Ruger Street

www.presidiosocialclub.com

A casual American restaurant with good food in an old military barracks with a great outdoor deck in a woodsy setting.

Hong Kong Lounge II

3300 Geary Boulevard

www.hongkonglounge2.com

Excellent dim sum during the day and Hong Kong seafood specialties at night.

R&G Lounge

631 Kearny Street

www.rnglounge.com

The specialty of this busy place on the edge of Chinatown is salt and pepper crab.

Zarzuela

2000 Hyde Street

This tapas restaurant in Russian Hill serves first-rate paella, meatballs, empanadas, gazpacho, and grilled squid.

Turtle Tower

645 Larkin Street

www.turtletowersf.com

A Vietnamese restaurant on the edge of the Tenderloin serving pho, noodle dishes, rice plates, and banh mi sandwiches.

Sites

The Palace of Fine Arts

3301 Lyon Street and Marina Boulevard

https://palaceoffinearts.org

This is the only surviving palace of the ten built for the Pan-Pacific Exposition of 1915. The original palace was framed in wood and covered in plaster, and was deteriorating when it was reconstructed in 1964.

Coit Tower

1 Telegraph Hill Blvd

http://sfrecpark.org/destination/telegraph-hill-pioneer-park/coit-tower/

The views from the top of this Art Deco tower are terrific; the New Deal murals inside are even better.

Sutro Heights Park

846 Point Lobos Avenue

The 18-acre (7-ha) park was originally a mansion with expansive gardens on a bluff overlooking Ocean Beach, Seal Rocks, and the Pacific. The Sutro family donated the estate to the city in 1938.

Heron's Head Park

Jennings Street and Cargo Way

http://sfport.com/herons-head-park

This narrow spit of a park juts into the bay from a shoreline once filled with piers, power plants, dry docks, and waterfront industries. Now it offers great views of the bay, of the city, and of wintering birds.

Union Square

Post and Powell Streets

www.unionsquareshop.com

The area surrounding the handsome plaza is filled with hotels, department stores, high-end boutiques, art galleries, restaurants, cafés, and the city's main theaters—the Geary, the Curran, and the Golden Gate.

Hunters Point Shipyard Artists

Horn Avenue

www.shipyardartists.com

Located on the former site of the u.s. naval shipyard at Hunter's Point, this is one of the oldest (since 1983) and largest (250 working studios) artist communities in the United States. The artists open their studios free of charge to the public during weekends in the spring and autumn.

Alcatraz Island

San Francisco Bay

www.nps.gov/alca/index.htm

You can take a tour of this former penitentiary that sits on a big rock in the bay and affords magnificent views of the bridges and the city.

Crissy Field

Old Mason Street and Marina Boulevard

www.parksconservancy.org/visit/park-sites/crissy-field.html

This former airfield was converted into a glorious ribbon park along the city's north shore. You can walk along the bay for a mile and a half (2.5 km) to Fort Point, stand almost directly underneath the Golden Gate Bridge and enjoy wide, open, and spectacular views.

The Castro Theatre

429 Castro Street

www.castrotheatre.com

Its ornate marquee, tall neon sign, and Mexican-cathedral facade make the Castro Theatre instantly recognizable. The theater specializes in repertory cinema and film festivals.

Middle Harbor Shoreline Park

2777 Middle Harbor Road, Oakland

www.portofoakland.com/port/seaport/middle-harbor

Built on the site of a former naval supply depot in Oakland, this park offers views of the bay, the city of San Francisco, and the bridges. You can get very close to tall cranes loading and unloading massive container ships, and see all manner of birds in winter.

Stores

Nijiya Market

1737 Post Street

www.nijiya.com

This Japanese supermarket in Japantown's Kintetsu Mall—which holds dozens of Japanese stores—offers bento boxes, sushi rolls, and donburi bowls, as well as Japanese vegetables, meats, and condiments.

Biordi Art Imports

412 Columbus Avenue

www.biordi.com

A museum-like store full of hand-painted ceramics in Maiolica (Italian Renaissance) style from Siena, Pesaro, Vietri, and Caltagirone.

Cheese Board Pizza

1512 Shattuck Avenue, Berkeley
www.cheeseboardcollective.coop
The Cheese Board has been a worker-owned business since 1971 and
offers 400 cheeses, delicious pizzas, and a big selection of fresh-baked
pastries and breads.

Cookin'

339 Divisadero Street
A vintage kitchen shop filled with old latte bowls, *Time/Life* cookbooks,
Le Creuset pots, handsome wooden spoons, hand-turned meat
grinders—just about every type of cookware imaginable.

Amoeba Records

2455 Telegraph Avenue, Berkeley
1855 Haight Street
www.amoeba.com
Amoeba first opened in 1990 on Telegraph Avenue in Berkeley, and
soon opened a store in a converted bowling alley on Haight Street in San
Francisco. Amoeba has a huge collection of new and used vinyl records
and CDs.

Monterey Market

1550 Hopkins Street, Berkeley
www.montereymarket.com
Even *New York Times* food writer Mark Bittman couldn't believe the
high quality, wide variety, and low price of fruit and produce at this
splendidly simple market run by the Fujimoto family since 1961.

Green Apple Books

506 Clement Street
www.greenapplebooks.com
A terrific neighborhood bookstore founded in 1967 with a large selection
that is nicely balanced between used and new books.

City Lights Bookstore

261 Columbus Avenue

www.citylights.com

A cornerstone for the Beats, and the entire North Beach neighborhood, since it was opened in 1953 by Lawrence Ferlinghetti and Peter Martin.

Moe's Books

2476 Telegraph Avenue, Berkeley

www.moesbooks.com

For a half-century now, Moe's has been selling used books at attractive prices to students and faculty at University of California, Berkeley, and to readers across the Bay Area.

William Stout Architectural Books

804 Montgomery Street, Jackson Square

www.stoutbooks.com

Perhaps the country's very best book store for architecture, city history, and urbanism.

Chronology

1776 The Spanish mission San Francisco de Asís is founded on the future Mission District of San Francisco

1846 American sailors raise their flag in the square of the forlorn Mexican outpost Yerba Buena to claim it for the United States

1848 Gold is discovered on the south fork of the American River

1849 San Francisco has 25,000 (mostly male) residents

1851 The first Vigilance Committee tries to impose order on the wild frontier town

1860 The Pony Express begins service from San Francisco to St Joseph, Missouri. A telegraph line connects San Francisco to Los Angeles

1865 The *Examiner* and the *Chronicle* begin publication

1869 The intercontinental railroad ties San Francisco to the rest of the country

1870 The future Golden Gate Park is created by an Act of the state legislature

1873 The first cable car climbs Nob Hill. The first Levi jeans are sold

1882 The Chinese Exclusion Act prevents Chinese laborers from coming to the United States

1896 Sutro Baths open on a bluff above the Pacific Ocean

1898   The (second and current) Ferry Building opens on the
        Embarcadero

1901   The working-class Union Labor Party becomes the first and
        only labor party to win control of a city government in the
        United States

1906   A major earthquake sets off a firestorm that destroys most of the
        eastern half of the city

1908   The Alcatraz cell-house is built

1912   James Rolph starts his twenty-year stretch as city mayor and
        oversees a sustained period of rapid growth, great prosperity,
        and high style

1915   The Pan-Pacific International Exposition, also known as the
        World's Fair, celebrates the opening of the Panama Canal
        and San Francisco's recovery from the earthquake. The first
        transcontinental telephone conversation takes place between
        New York and San Francisco

1933   Coit Tower is officially dedicated

1934   In the middle of the Depression, a waterfront strike dominates
        the city's life for three months. After two decades of construc-
        tion, drinking water from Hetch Hetchy Reservoir reaches San
        Francisco

1936/7 The Bay Bridge and the Golden Gate Bridge open

1938   Herb Caen starts writing what will be the longest-running
        newspaper column in the country, totaling some 16,000
        columns of 1,000 words about San Francisco

1941–5   The Second World War effectively ends the Depression in San Francisco by making the Bay Area the Pacific theater's premier command and supply center

1943   The Chinese Exclusion Act is repealed

1957   The New York Giants move to San Francisco

1966   The Beatles play their last live concert, at Candlestick Park

1967   The Human Be-in at Golden Gate Park shows the hippies to the world

1972   BART (Bay Area Rapid Transit) connects San Francisco to the east bay and to the rest of the peninsula

1978   Former supervisor Dan White shoots and kills Supervisor Harvey Milk and Mayor George Moscone in City Hall

1989   A big earthquake shakes the city and leads to the tearing-down of the Embarcadero freeway

2004   San Francisco starts issuing same-sex marriage licenses

2006   Twitter founded and headquartered in San Francisco

2009   Uber founded and headquartered in San Francisco

2016   Both U.S. senators from California, Dianne Feinstein and Kamala Harris, are San Franciscans

2017   The shiny, conical, 1,070-foot Salesforce.com skyscraper looms over downtown and can be seen from all across the city and Bay Area.

Suggested Reading and Viewing

Ackley, Laura, *San Francisco's Jewel City: The Panama-Pacific International Exposition of 1915* (Berkeley, CA, 2014)

Altrocchi, Julia, *The Spectacular San Franciscans* (New York, 1949)

Asbury, Herbert, *The Barbary Coast: An Informal History of the San Francisco Underworld* (New York, 1933)

Atherton, Edwin, "Atherton Report on Graft in the San Francisco Police Department," *San Francisco Examiner* (March 17, 1937)

Bakalinsky, Adah, *Stairway Walks in San Francisco* (San Francisco, CA, 1984)

Baker Barnhart, Jacqueline, *The Fair but Frail: Prostitution in San Francisco, 1849–1900* (Reno, NV, 1986)

Barker, Malcolm, ed., *San Francisco Memoirs, 1835–1851: Eyewitness Accounts of the Birth of a City* (San Francisco, CA, 1994)

—, ed., *More San Francisco Memoirs, 1852–1899: The Ripening Years* (San Francisco, CA, 1996)

Barnes, Merritt, "'Fountainhead of Corruption': Peter P. McDonough, Boss of San Francisco's Underworld," *California History*, 2 (Summer 1979), pp. 142–53

Barth, Gunther, *Instant Cities: Urbanization and the Rise of San Francisco and Denver* (New York, 1975)

Bean, Walton, *Boss Ruef's San Francisco: The Story of the Union Labor Party, Big Business, and the Graft Prosecution* (Berkeley, CA, 1952)

Beebe, Lucius, *San Francisco's Golden Era: A Picture Story of San Francisco before the Fire* (Berkeley, CA, 1960)

Benemann, William, ed., *A Year of Mud and Gold: San Francisco in Letters and Diaries, 1849–1850* (Lincoln, NE, 1999)

Berglund, Barbara, *Making San Francisco American: Cultural Frontiers in the Urban West, 1846–1906* (Lawrence, KS, 2007)

Bronstein, Zelda, "How Silicon Valley Millionaires Stole Progressivism," *The Nation* (July 15, 2014)

Broussard, Albert, *Black San Francisco: The Struggle for Racial Equality in the West* (Lawrence, KS, 1993)

Burgess, Gelett, *The Heart Line: A Drama of San Francisco* (San Francisco, CA, 1907)

Caen, Herb, *Baghdad by the Bay* (New York, 1949)

—, with photographer Max Yavno, *The San Francisco Book* (Boston, MA, 1948)

—, *The Best of Herb Caen, 1960–1975* (San Francisco, CA, 1991)

Chamber of Commerce, *Handbook for San Francisco* (San Francisco, CA, 1914)

Chen, Yong, *Chinese San Francisco: 1850–1943* (Stanford, CA, 2000)

Cherny, Robert, *Victor Arnautoff and the Politics of Art* (Champaign, IL, 2017)

—, and William Issel, *San Francisco, 1865–1932: Politics, Power, and Urban Development* (Berkeley, CA, 1986)

Cross, Ira, *A History of the Labor Movement in California* (Berkeley, CA, 1935)

De Massey, Ernest, *A Frenchman in the Gold Rush: The Journal of Ernest de Massey, Argonaut of 1849* (San Francisco, CA, 1927)

Densmore, G. B., *The Chinese in California: Description of Chinese Life in San Francisco* (San Francisco, CA, 1880)

Didion, Joan, *Slouching Towards Bethlehem* (New York, 1968)

Dobie, Charles, *San Francisco: A Pageant* (New York, 1933)

Edwords, Clarence, *Bohemian San Francisco* (San Francisco, CA, 1914)

Ehrlich, Jake, *A Life in My Hands* (New York, 1965)

Eliel, Paul, *The Waterfront and General Strikes, San Francisco, 1934* (San Francisco, CA, 1934)

Fallon, Michael, "A New Paradise for Beatniks," *San Francisco Examiner* (September 5, 1965)

Fardon, George, *San Francisco Album: Photographs of the Most Beautiful Views and Public Buildings of San Francisco* (San Francisco, CA, 1856)

Gilliam, Harold, *The Face of San Francisco* (New York, 1960)

Hammett, Dashiell, *The Maltese Falcon* (New York, 1929)

Hellman, Lillian, "Dashiell Hammett: A Memoir," *New York Review of Books* (November 25, 1965)

Hinckle, Warren, "The Social History of the Hippies," *Ramparts* (March 1967), pp. 5–26

Hippler, Arthur, *Hunter's Point: A Black Ghetto* (New York, 1974)

Hopper, James, "Our San Francisco," *Everybody's Magazine* (June 1906)

Howell, Ocean, *Making the Mission: Planning and Ethnicity in San Francisco* (Chicago, IL, 2015)

Irwin, Will, *The City That Was: A Requiem of Old San Francisco* (San Francisco, CA, 1906)

—, ed., *Old Chinatown: A Book of Pictures by Arnold Genthe* (New York, 1908)

Jackson, Charles Tenney, *The Day of Souls* (Indianapolis, IN, 1910)

Johns, Michael, "Winning for Losing: A New Look at Harry Bridges and the 'Big Strike' of 1934," *American Communist History*, XIII/1 (2014), pp. 1–24

Johns, Orrick, *Time of Our Lives* (New York, 1937)

Kahn, Judd, *Imperial San Francisco: Politics and Planning in an American City, 1897–1906* (Lincoln, NE, 1979)

Kamiya, Gary, *Cool Grey City of Love: 49 Views of San Francisco* (New York, 2013)

Kazin, Michael, *Barons of Labor: The San Francisco Building Trades and Union Power in the Progressive Era* (Urbana, IL, 1987)

Kerouac, Jack, "Aftermath: The Philosophy of the Beat Generation," *Esquire* (March 1958)

—, *The Subterraneans* (New York, 1958)

Knapp, Henry, *Chinatown* (San Francisco, CA, 1889)

Lewis, Oscar, *The Big Four: The Story of Huntington, Stanford, Hopkins and Crocker* (New York, 1938)

—, *Bay Window Bohemia: An Account of the Brilliant Artistic World of Gaslit San Francisco* (New York, 1956)

Lloyd, B. E., *Lights and Shades in San Francisco* (San Francisco, CA, 1876)

London, Jack, "South of the Slot," *Saturday Evening Post* (May 22, 1909)

Lotchin, Roger, *San Francisco, 1846–1856: From Hamlet to City* (New York, 1974)

Lyndon, Michael, "An Evening with the Grateful Dead," *Rolling Stone* (September 17, 1970)

Maupin, Armistead, *Tales of the City* (New York, 1978)

Meltzer, David, *San Francisco Beat: Talking with the Poets* (San Francisco, CA, 2001)

Mencken, H. L., "San Francisco: A Memory," *Baltimore Evening Sun* (July 21, 1920)

—, "Romantic Intermezzo," in *Heathen Days, 1890–1936* (New York, 1943)

Minton, Bruce, and John Stuart, *Men Who Lead Labor* (New York, 1937)

Mullen, Kevin, *Let Justice Be Done: Crime and Politics in Early San Francisco* (Reno, NV, 1989)

Norris, Frank, *McTeague* (San Francisco, CA, 1899)

—, *The Octopus: A Story of California* (New York, 1903)

—, *Blix* (New York, 1925)

—, *Frank Norris of "The Wave": Stories and Sketches from the San Francisco Weekly, 1893–1897* (San Francisco, CA, 1931)

O'Connell, Daniel, *The Inner Man: Good Things to Eat and Drink and Where to Get Them* (San Francisco, CA, 1891)

O'Shaughnessy, Michael, *Hetch Hetchy: Its Origin and History* (San Francisco, CA, 1934)

Parkinson, Thomas, *A Casebook on the Beat* (New York, 1961)

Peixotto, Ernest, "Architecture in San Francisco," *The Overland Monthly* (May 1893), pp. 449–61

Perry, Charles, *The Haight-Ashbury: A History* (New York, 1984)

Pfeiffer, Ida, *A Lady's Visit to California, 1853* (Oakland, CA, 1950)

Pollock, Christopher, *San Francisco's Golden Gate Park: A Thousand and Seventeen Acres of Stories* (Portland, OR, 2001)

Rabb, Earl, "There's No City Like San Francisco," *Commentary* (October 1950), pp. 369–78

Rexroth, Kenneth, "San Francisco Letter," *The Evergreen Review*, 1/2 (1957), pp. 5–14

Richards, Rand, *Mud, Blood, and Gold: San Francisco in 1849* (San Francisco, CA, 2009)

Richardson, Peter, *No Simple Highway: A Cultural History of the Grateful Dead* (New York, 2015)

Rischin, Moses, "Sunny Jim Rolph: The First 'Mayor of the People'," *California Historical Quarterly* (Summer 1974), pp. 165–72

Rodriguez, Richard, "Late Victorians," in *Days of Obligation: An Argument with My Mexican Father* (New York, 1992)

Rolling Stone: The Fortieth Anniversary (July 12–26, 2007)

Schaeffer, L. M., *Sketches of Travels in South America, Mexico and California* (New York, 1860)

Selvin, David, *A Terrible Anger: The 1934 Waterfront and General Strikes in San Francisco* (Detroit, MI, 1996)

Seth, Vikram, *The Golden Gate* (New York, 1986)

Shaw, Randy, *The Tenderloin: Sex, Crime, and Resistance in the Heart of San Francisco* (San Francisco, CA, 2015)

Shilts, Randy, *And the Band Played On: Politics, People, and the AIDS Epidemic* (New York, 1987)

——, *The Mayor of Castro Street: The Life and Times of Harvey Milk* (New York, 1982)

Sides, Josh, *Erotic City: Sexual Revolutions and the Making of Modern San Francisco* (New York, 2009)

Solnit, Rebecca, *Infinite City: A San Francisco Atlas* (Berkeley, CA, 2010)

Soulé, Frank, et al., *The Annals of San Francisco* (Palo Alto, CA, 1966; originally published New York, 1855)

Starr, Kevin, "Baghdad by the Bay," in *Golden Dreams: California in the Age of Abundance* (New York, 2009)

Talbot, David, *Season of the Witch: Enchantment, Terror, and Deliverance in the City of Love* (New York, 2012)

Tausanovitch, Chris, and Christopher Warshaw, "Representation in Municipal Government," *American Political Science Review*, CVIII/3 (2014), pp. 605–41

Taylor, Bayard, *Eldorado: or, Adventures in the Path of Empire* (New York, 1850)

Thompson, Hunter S., "The 'Hashbury' is the Capital of the Hippies," *New York Times Magazine* (May 14, 1967)

Thoreau, Henry David, "Life without Principle", *Atlantic Monthly* (October 1863), pp. 484–94

Walsh, James, "Abe Ruef Was No Boss: Machine Politics, Reform, and San Francisco," *California Historical Quarterly* (Spring 1972), pp. 3–16

Webb, Beatrice, *American Diary, 1898* (Madison, WI, 1963)

Weller, Sheila, "Suddenly That Summer," *Vanity Fair* (June 14, 2012)

Williams, Samuel, "The City of the Golden Gate," *Scribner's Monthly* (July 1875), pp. 266–85

Wolfe, Tom, *The Electric Kool-aid Acid Test* (New York, 1968)

Movies

After the Thin Man, dir. W. S. Van Dyke (1936)

Bullitt, dir. Peter Yates (1968)

The Conversation, dir. Francis Ford Coppola (1974)

Dark Passage, dir. Delmer Daves (1947)

Days of Wine and Roses, dir. Blake Edwards (1962)

Dirty Harry, dir. Don Siegel (1971)

Guess Who's Coming to Dinner, dir. Stanley Kramer (1967)

Invasion of the Body Snatchers, dir. Philip Kaufman (1978)

The Joy Luck Club, dir. Wayne Wang (1993)

The Line-up, dir. Don Siegel (1958)

Madams of the Barbary Coast, dir. Michael Rohde (2008)

Magnum Force, dir. Ted Post (1973)

The Maltese Falcon, dir. John Huston (1941)

Mrs. Doubtfire, dir. Chris Columbus (1994)

Petulia, dir. Richard Lester (1968)

The Times of Harvey Milk, dir. Rob Epstein (1984)

The Towering Inferno, dir. John Guillermin (1974)

Vertigo, dir. Alfred Hitchcock (1958)

The Wild Parrots of Telegraph Hill, dir. Judy Irving (2003)

Photo Acknowledgments

The author and publishers wish to express their thanks to the below sources of illustrative material and/or permission to reproduce it.

Theresa Cho: pp. 10 bottom, 13; iStockphoto: pp. 8 top (holgs), 10 top (rramirez125), 130 (EddieHernandezPhotography), 142 (yhelfman); Michael Johns: pp. 6, 14, 43, 55, 80, 85, 129, 131, 132, 141, 148–9, 154, 155, 157, 158, 159, 163, 166, 168, 170, 171, 172, 173, 176, 178, 179, 182, 185, 186, 188, 189, 190, 194, 195, 196, 197, 198; Mary Anne Kramer: p. 117; Sonia Lehman-Frisch: pp. 144, 151, 199; Library of Congress Prints and Photographs Division: pp. 20, 23, 47, 49, 59, 93; Oakland Museum of California: pp. 31, 58, 74, 79, 84, 86; David Rumsey: pp. 40–41, 64; *San Francisco Examiner*: p. 122; San Francisco History Center, San Francisco Public Library: pp. 19 (Dennis L. Maness Summer of Love Collection), 29, 31, 32, 34, 36, 39, 42, 44, 45, 48, 52, 62, 65, 66, 69, 70, 84 top, 88, 90, 94, 96–7, 100, 105, 106, 107, 108, 111, 112, 113, 114, 115, 118, 123, 125, 136; Shutterstock/Koby Dagan: p. 7; Shutterstock/Bill Perry: p. 12; unsplash.com: pp. 8 bottom (Peter Boccia), 9 (Sasha, instagram.com/sanfrancisco), 11 (Pedro Lastra), 143 (Patrick Gothe).

Index

Page numbers in *italics* refer to illustrations